AF886103

THE NATIVE AMERICAN *Dream*

What people are saying about *The Native American Dream*

"An impressively thorough work and a necessary read. The forward-looking perspective of Chapter 7 truly resonates with me—illustrating how authors must envision the future as they craft their narratives. It's a highly ambitious and commendable approach, encouraging readers to not only reflect on history but to actively engage with the future."

—Speaker Emeritus Anthony Rendon, California State Assembly

"I've never experienced a book quite like *The Native American Dream* by Dr. Rod Wilson. From cover to cover, it held me in its grip, compelling me to turn page after page in eager anticipation of what would come next. Truly riveting and accurate history of our people!"

—Elaine Whitehurst, Shingle Springs Band of Miwok Indians Development Corporation, Board Member

"This book masterfully weaves the narrative of our people, highlighting our resilience and the importance of preserving tribal sovereignty for future generations."

—Erica M. Pinto, Chairwoman, Jamul Indian Village

"This book masterfully clarifies the complex narrative of tribal governments, urging a deeper respect and understanding crucial for our times."

—California State Assemblymember James C. Ramos, San Manuel Band of Mission Indians Tribal Member

"While Native American Tribal Sovereignty is guaranteed at the federal level, Native American tribal Prosperity depends on smart and unrelenting political and economic initiatives at the state and county level. Rod Wilson's masterful book, *The Native American Dream*, details how innovative Tribes have won those battles, thereby guaranteeing prosperity and self-reliance not only for themselves but for their non-Native neighbors, too."

***—Sean Flynn, Ph.D., Dept. of Economics, Scripps College and Author of* Economics for Dummies**

"I bring a distinctive perspective serving both local government entities and a tribal government over the last four decades and understand the necessity of recognizing and understanding the nuances of tribal sovereignty. *The Native American Dream* is an essential guide for anyone engaged in public service. This book brilliantly unfolds the complex layers of tribal sovereignty and offers invaluable insights into collaborating with tribal governments. A comprehensive historical context yet grounded in contemporary relevance. It goes beyond the theoretical, providing practical guidance for fostering respectful partnerships with tribal nations. I believe it should be a staple in the libraries of government offices nationwide."

—G. Michael Milhiser, Retired Chief Administrative Officer, Morongo Band of Mission Indians

THE NATIVE AMERICAN *Dream*

Beating the Odds in the Fight for Self-Reliance

ROD WILSON, PH.D.

Claremont Graduate University
Claremont, California

The Native American Dream

Some research conducted at the Drucker School of Management
Claremont Graduate University

Library of Congress Control Number: 2023919907

ISBN 979-8-9892523-1-2 (hardcover)
ISBN 979-8-9892523-0-5 (paperback)
ISBN 979-8-9892523-2-9 (ebook)

Book Design: Clarity Designworks

Printed in the United States of America

DrRodWilson.com

This book honors the path forged by California's Native American ancestors. Their wisdom and resilience have taught all humanity the virtues of courage in the face of adversity, creating a legacy of self-reliance. Their stories, rich with lessons and sacrifices, inspire a commitment to a better future. It is to their indomitable spirit and deep-seated dedication to subsequent generations that this work is respectfully dedicated.

About the Cover

The cover showcases the vibrant heritage and governance of Native American tribes, set against the expanding backdrop of neighboring communities which have grown up around reservations. This representation honors the resilience and evolution of tribal societies, prompting a journey through the interwoven stories of age-old customs and their place in today's world.

Contents

CHAPTER FIVE

CHAPTER SIX

CHAPTER SEVEN

EPILOGUE

ABOUT THE AUTHOR

The Fight for Self-Reliance

The opening pages of this book explore the vital theme of tribal self-reliance, a central focus that runs through the heart of the stories we're about to explore. Before we journey further, let's pause to grasp the profound significance of self-reliance. Understanding this theme will enrich your appreciation of the tribes' struggles and the decisions that shaped their destinies.

The Road to Self-Reliance:

In the intricate mosaic of Native American history and culture, the concept of self-reliance transcends mere economic autonomy; it embodies the very essence of survival, resilience, and cultural preservation. The journey towards self-reliance for Native American tribes is a testament to their enduring spirit, unyielding determination, and unwavering commitment to reclaim their rightful place in the story of America.

A Legacy of Survival:

For centuries, Native American communities have navigated a complex and often turbulent path. They have faced the ravages of colonization, endured the loss of ancestral lands, and weathered the storm of historical injustices. Yet, at the core of this tumultuous history lies an indomitable spirit that refuses to be extinguished.

The drive for self-reliance is deeply intertwined with the survival of Native American cultures. It is a response to centuries of adversity, a promise to future generations that their heritage will not only endure but thrive. Self-reliance, for Native Americans, means the ability to protect and perpetuate their unique traditions, languages, and identities.

Beyond Economics:

While economic self-sufficiency is undoubtedly a critical component of self-reliance, it extends far beyond financial independence. It encompasses the capacity to govern, educate, and heal their communities, all rooted in their own cultural values and wisdom. Self-reliance empowers tribes to make decisions that best serve their members, unburdened by external influences that may not fully comprehend their unique needs.

The Battle Against Stereotypes:

One of the significant challenges that Native American communities face is the pervasive cloud of stereotypes and misconceptions that often shroud their efforts towards self-reliance. These stereotypes paint a distorted picture of tribes solely as recipients of governmental aid or as profit-driven entities through endeavors like Indian gaming.

The truth is that self-reliance is the antidote to these misrepresentations. It is how Native American communities dispel these myths and showcase their resilience, creativity, and cultural richness. Their journey towards self-reliance is a powerful rebuttal to the outdated narratives that have for too long defined their image in the eyes of the wider world.

The Vision of Self-Determination:

Self-reliance and self-determination are inextricably linked. To be self-reliant is to exercise the inherent right to self-governance, a right recognized and protected by the U.S. Constitution, treaties, and federal laws. Achieving self-reliance means breaking free from the paternalistic shackles of the past, where decisions were made for Native American communities rather than with them.

RECOGNIZED TRIBES IN
CALIFORNIA
Smith River
Elk Valley
Big Lagoon
Trinidad
Yurok
Hoopa
Karuk
Quartz Valley
Karuk
XL Ranch
Fort Bidwell
Cedarville
Alturas
Lookout
Likely
Blue Lake
Table Bluff
Rohnerville
Big Bend
Roaring Creek
Montgomery Creek
Pit River
Redding Rancheria
Susanville
Greenville
Susanville
Round Valley
Laytonville
Sherwood Valley
Paskenta
Chico Rancheria
Grindstone
Berry Creek
Coyote Valley
Redwood Valley
Enterprise
Mooretown
Pinoleville
Upper Lake
Colusa
Manchester
Robinson
Cortina
Guidiville
Sulphur Bank
Hopland
Rumsey
Stewarts Point
Big Valley
Cloverdale
Middletown
Dry Creek
Graton
Lytton
Wade Parcels
Washoe (Woodfords Community)
Springs
Ione Band
Jackson
Sheep Ranch
Me-Wuk
Bridgeport
Tuolumne
Chicken Ranch
Benton Paiute
Picayune
North Fork
Bishop
Big Sandy
Big Pine
Table Mountain
Cold Springs
Fort Independence
Lone Pine
Timbisha Homelands
Santa Rosa
Tule River
Santa Ynez
Fort Mojave
Chemehuevi
San Manuel
Morongo
Twenty-Nine Palms
Soboba
Agua Caliente
Santa Rosa
Cabazon
Colorado River
Ramona
Augustine
Cahuilla
Cabazon
Pechanga
Torres-Martinez
Pala
Pauma-Yuima
Los Coyotes
San Pasqual
Santa Ysabel
Mesa Grande
Inaja-Cosmit
Barona
Capitan Grande
Viejas
Cuyapaipe
Quechan
Sycuan
Manzanita
Jamul Indian Village
La Posta
Campo
5
80
5
5
40
15
10
15

A Call for Understanding:

This book serves as a lens through which we can explore the multifaceted journey of Native American tribes towards self-reliance. It invites readers to challenge preconceptions, dispel stereotypes, and embark on a journey of understanding and respect. It illuminates the complex landscape of history, culture, and resilience that defines the Native American experience.

The stories shared within these pages are not just narratives of economic progress; they are chronicles of survival, identity reclamation, and the relentless pursuit of self-determination. They underscore the importance of acknowledging the rich diversity of Native American cultures and the profound significance of their journey towards self-reliance.

As you begin this book, it's important to recognize that tribal governments are acknowledged by the federal government as democratic entities. Each tribe operates autonomously, guided by its unique tribal constitution. Tribal leadership, including positions like Chairman, Chairwoman, Vice-Chairman, Secretary, and others, is elected by eligible members within the tribe. Throughout this book, you'll encounter these titles, reflecting the roles of various individuals who were elected at different times to represent their tribal communities during the historical events discussed.

As we delve into the lives and struggles of these communities, let us remember that their journey is not just theirs; it is a shared journey towards a more inclusive, equitable, and understanding society. The time for understanding is now. Join us on this voyage of revelation and appreciation.

Introduction

In a nation known for its resilience and victories, some stories remain silent, voices unheard, and experiences unknown. Many ignore or misunderstand the deep history, challenges, and enduring spirit of America's first inhabitants. These stories aren't just side notes; they're central to our shared history, deserving recognition, understanding, and respect.

In a landscape where solutions often seem superficial and reactive, tribal communities stand as luminous examples of determination, vision, and unwavering spirit. Their journey is not just about monetary prosperity, but a testament to the strength of the human spirit. Their struggles, dreams, and the road to self-reliance are carved amidst formidable challenges, distinct in character, yet resonating with the ideals of the American Dream.

Understanding these narratives is more than a pursuit of historical knowledge. It gives witness to our shared humanity and recognizes the legacies that have shaped our present. To ignore or sideline these accounts is to deny ourselves a deeper understanding of the forces that have shaped our nation.

Alexis de Tocqueville's observation during his 1830s visit to the United States poignantly applies to my experiences with Native American communities over three decades. These tribes, representing America's first associations, stood united in shared values, intent on self-sustainability, and a dedication to preserving a rich heritage that precedes modern America.

Beginning with a simple cold call to a tribe in San Bernardino, my journey unveiled a realm of challenges and triumphs that few recognize and far fewer understand. Through this association, I saw firsthand the battles tribes faced, both internal and external. Legal confrontations, societal misjudgments, financial burdens, and more stood as hurdles, but their spirit never wavered.

This book tells the stories of three tribes, shedding light on the resilience of tribal leaders, their belief in sovereignty, and their dreams for their community. They've faced challenges, but in their victories, they've not grown bitter. Instead, they've emerged as community leaders and key contributors to the broader societal narrative of America.

These stories hold vital lessons for all of humanity. For the sake of understanding, for the importance of preserving history, and for the betterment of our shared future, it is time these narratives are known. Dive into these pages to discover a world rarely acknowledged but teeming with inspiration.

Native American tribes represent a wealth of history often overlooked in common narratives. Their journey is filled with intrigue, drama, and profound human experiences. With 109 federally recognized tribes, California stands as a beacon of diverse cultures and languages unmatched in any other state.

But this is no ordinary recounting of facts. This is an exploration, as intimate as it is intense, into the very core of three of these tribes: the San Manuel Band of Mission Indians, the Jamul Indian Village, and the Shingle Springs Band of Miwok Indians.

Can you imagine a journey from abject poverty to the glittering lights of affluence, all within a span of three decades? An aspiration for a dream deemed unreachable. These tribes not only imagined it but traversed this challenging path, while facing monumental adversities. This is their story.

The late 20th century found Californians in blissful ignorance, unaware of the shadows of a harrowing past. California's tribes, first recognized in the 1850's, were ironically acknowledged in a manner that spelt their doom. The paradox of their recognition was painfully clear: they were seen but not valued.

From once ruling their ancestral land, they were displaced to inhospitable terrains, made victims of broken treaties and unspeakable injustices. But perhaps what stands out the most is how their very source of new empowerment, the casino gaming, came with its own set of ironies. While the government allowed them the means to uplift themselves, it also shackled them by dictating their expenditures and restrictions placed on tribal governments.

And just when the tribes sought to rise, giants of industry, from Wynn to Caesars, tried pulling them down, lest they share the American Dream with the very people on whose lands the dream was built.

But as I've learned over three decades, the spirit of these tribes is unyielding. Their aspiration is not born from victimhood but from a burning desire for autonomy, dignity, and a rightful place in the American story.

In the following chapters, I peel back the layers of time, revealing dialogues, decisions, and moments that defined these tribes. While some led to victories and others to defeats, each moment has sculpted their destiny, reminding us of the tenacity and resilience of America's first inhabitants.

Dive deeper, not only to uncover an obscured chapter of history but also to feel the pulse of a people who, against formidable odds, opted to ascend, flourish, and transmit an enduring legacy. Let their stories invigorate and entice you deeper into their world.

In the upcoming sections, I will guide you through accounts that collectively shape the vast American landscape. These serve as mere glimpses into narratives that underscore the unyielding determination, fortitude, and foresight of Native American tribes on their path to self-sufficiency.

Think for a moment about the widely recognized fear of public speaking. Studies tell us that an overwhelming 87% would rather have their fingernails pulled out than stand and speak before an audience. It's a sentiment that cuts across cultures and backgrounds. Now, imagine Native American tribal leaders, many stepping away from their reservations for the very first time, confronting this fear. Their courage, not just in overcoming this anxiety but in harnessing the transformative power of their voice, serves as a beacon of inspiration for anyone who has ever felt the weight of self-doubt.

This story shows tribal members stepping into the fast-paced political world of Sacramento and Washington D.C. for the first time. The bustling Capitols were a stark contrast to their homes and life on the reservation. Yet, each trip and conversation with an official was a step towards building bridges and making their voices heard.

With the establishment of the statewide organization, CNIGA, in Sacramento, tribes weren't just staking a claim in political dialogues; they were laying the groundwork for a collective future. The tales detail how, from being novices in the complex dance of politics, they became its choreographers. Their swift ascent, from political outsiders to influential players, is unparalleled. They didn't merely adapt to the rules of the game; they reshaped them.

While the journey to legalize Indian gaming in California involved thousands of individuals, this book takes a more nuanced approach, spotlighting the experiences of three tribes. Rather than delving into the intricacies of Proposition 5 or Proposition 1A, its primary focus is on how these tribes leveraged those endeavors to safeguard their tribal sovereignty. The intention is not in any way to diminish the contributions of countless others but to offer a deeper understanding of the unique challenges and choices faced by these tribes on their path to self-reliance.

These stories, and the many more that follow, aren't just historical accounts. They are testimonies to the indomitable spirit of a people who, when faced with adversity, chose to rise. And in their ascent, they've sketched a compelling blueprint for resilience, unity, and vision. So, as you turn the pages, be prepared to be inspired, awed, and reminded of the power of determination and what you can do in the face of adversity.

It's time to introduce some of the players:

In Sacramento, it was the leadership and members of the Latino Caucus that quickly understood the struggles and challenges the tribes faced. They stood firm as allies, championing the tribes' drive for independence. This bond cut across race, politics, and money and was component of the overall success in Sacramento.

In the 1960s, a twist of fate left the Shingle Springs Band of Miwok Indians isolated. California's realignment and expansion of Highway 50 turned their reservation into an unintended island. The tribe was forced into a legal maze: they needed to change laws to be able to talk to Caltrans just to regain a path home. Considering the state's contentious history with tribes, a shadow of doubt hung heavy: was this isolation of the tribe a mere oversight or a deliberate act? Facing this veiled adversity, how would the tribe confront and surmount such an unforeseen obstacle? The answer was neither clear nor simple.

The tribe's quest for answers led them to Sacramento, wondering why Caltrans would not talk to them. With their lobbyist, the late Luisa Sustaita, and advice from their trusted advisor Rich Ritts, the tribe made the long drive to Sacramento weekly for three years. Shockingly, Caltrans' guidelines never acknowledged tribes or recognized them as legitimate governments. If it wasn't in their guidelines, Caltrans simply wouldn't do it. Trips to Sacramento turned out to be quite the workout for the tribe. Between 25 to 40 meetings a day meant tackling the State Capitol's notorious stairwells going from floor to floor. It wasn't long before they discovered that the real key to conquering Sacramento wasn't diplomacy — it was a good pair of sneakers!

During this time, the tribe dived deep into the world of legislation. They learned firsthand how a simple idea faces hurdles before turning into a law. The Latino Caucus, with standouts like Assemblyman Tony Cardenas, Chief of Staff Jose Cornejo, Senator Richard Polanco, Speaker Cruz Bustamante, Assemblyman Antonio Villaraigosa, and Assemblyman Joe Baca, were key supporters. Because of this strong support, Attorney General Bill Lockyer not only looked at the tribe's proposal but gave it his stamp of approval.

After a long and tiring 18 months, the tribe's hard work seemed to pay off. On the last day of the session, a key day for many bills, Elaine Whitehurst leading the group from Shingle Springs found herself waiting anxiously at the Capitol. Late at night, they got the news they hoped for: their bill had passed all the legal checks and got approval from both houses. But the celebration was short. Governor Davis surprised them by vetoing the bill.

This setback didn't stop them. They geared up for more trips to Sacramento in the next session, adding another 7,000 miles to their odometers, pushing for the changes they believed were right and gave them access to their reservation. After another tough legislative period spent educating members of the legislature about Caltrans, they, along with their supporters, waited again on the last night of the session. Their hard work and persistence finally won. Governor Gray Davis acknowledged the value of their efforts and signed the bill. This allowed Shingle Springs to work with Caltrans and ultimately build and pay for an access ramp to their land.

The tale of the Jamul Indian Village is one for the ages — arguably deserving the title for the longest and most challenging journey to open a casino.

San Diego County, with more tribes than any other county in the country, was a battleground for Jamul. They faced fierce resistance, notably from Supervisor Dianne Jacob. Surprisingly, Jacob was an Indian gaming supporter, but when it came to Jamul's casino, she fiercely proclaimed, "Not in my backyard!" Even going so far as to declare the casino would open "over her dead body." Yet, as time went on and term limits approached, she exited the stage. Despite her ardent opposition and more than 40 lawsuits from a local coalition in Jamul she supported and helped to spearhead, Jamul's determination remained unbroken.

Over two decades, the tribe showcased their resilience. They stood firm at community meetings, facing off against vocal opponents. Some of these detractors, who claimed to be well-educated and cultured, resorted to words so coarse they'd make a sailor blush. But through all the verbal assaults and legal challenges, Jamul stood tall. Drawing strength from their ancestral roots, and with critical guidance and support from tribal members Carlene Chamberlain, Bill Meza, Kenneth Mesa, Erica Pinto, and others they finally opened the doors to their casino. Their story stands as a testament: harsh words can wound, but unwavering spirit heals and prevails.

In an era marked by tribal disputes, some tribes and their consultants were inadvertently hindering their own progress. Recognizing this, the San Manuel Band of Mission Indians undertook extensive research and embarked on a mission to bring Indian gaming to the ballot, challenging the prevailing opinions.

Picture this: a tension-filled room in Sacramento's Hyatt, overflowing with tribal leaders and their consultants. A survey presentation hinted at a promising future for tribal gaming on reservations, but skeptics were many. Prominent among them was lobbyist Richie Ross, who was joined by many who expressed absolute doubt about the strategy. Voices rose, tempers flared, and the microphone became the center stage for passionate outbursts.

But amid the chaos, San Manuel's belief in their cause and the research never wavered. Jerry Levine, their tribal attorney, with an air of defiance, rolled up his sleeves and declared, "let's get this done!" The ensuing journey would see the creation of a tribal coalition unlike any before in its scale and ambition. Join us as we delve deeper into this pivotal moment in history.

Whet your appetite for a journey deep into California's heart, where the prospect of tribal gaming was beginning to shimmer with promise. Surveys showed Californians supporting the idea of tribal gaming on reservations. And tribes? They weren't just names or faces; they were the heartbeat of communities, creating jobs and driving local economies. Remarkably, Indian gaming was already the bread and butter for 50,000 souls and hundreds of local groups and organizations that relied upon their generosity to provide services to so many in local communities.

Enter San Manuel's grand bingo hall, a place that would soon echo with more than just the calls of bingo numbers. Members of the San Manuel Business Committee took center stage, with Chairman Henry Duro, Vice Chairman Ken Ramirez, Audrey Martinez, Lynn Valbuena, James Ramos and other prominent members sharing their fervent hopes and dreams. Surrounded by a sea of 3,000 employees and their families in the bingo hall, they painted a vivid picture of the potential and importance of Proposition 5.

Yet, this gathering was more than just heartfelt speeches. It was alive with celebration, energy, and unity. The air buzzed with enthusiasm, punctuated by the fun and laughter of Lynn Valbuena and Audrey Martinez leading the "chicken dance." It was a beautiful fusion of lighthearted fun and profound commitment. Attendees walked away with not just a spring in their step but also a deep-seated appreciation for the tribes' dedication to their community and a brighter shared future. Dive in with us to relive this captivating moment in history.

The path to tribal self-reliance has been fraught with challenges, from combating prejudices to navigating legal mazes. Yet, these tales aren't just of perseverance but of an unyielding spirit that refuses to dim. By delving into this history, we not only salute their resilience but also emphasize their rightful role in California's narrative of progress.

The struggle for tribal sovereignty is a relentless one, constantly engaged with political and legal adversities. Framing this complex discourse necessitates the collective wisdom of legal experts, political strategists, and seasoned jurists. Spearheaded by Chairman Deron Marquez of the San Manuel Band of Mission Indians, such gatherings are not just meetings of minds but are a testament to the tenacity and resilience in the pursuit of tribal autonomy and justice.

The landmark conference titled "Tribal Sovereignty: Legal Trends & Directions," co-hosted by the San Manuel Band of Mission Indians, the Foundation for California and Claremont Graduate University, served as a pivotal moment in the discussion of Native American tribal sovereignty. Held on March 12, 2008, in the esteemed halls of

The Catholic University of America Columbus School of Law, the event brought to the forefront the pressing issues surrounding tribal rights and governance.

The conference saw a gathering of the nation's foremost judicial and academic experts in federal Indian law, engaging in a series of panel discussions that delved into the intricacies of tribal sovereignty. Topics ranged from labor relations within tribal nations to legal precedents and strategies crucial for preserving tribal independence for generations to come.

Notable attendees included Ralph Rossum, Salvatori Professor of American Constitutionalism at Claremont McKenna College; The Honorable Susan A. Ehrlich of the Arizona Court of Appeals; The Honorable Rebecca Irving, Chief Judge of the Passamaquoddy Tribal Court; Kathryn R.L. Rand, Co-Director of the Institute for the Study of Tribal Gaming Law and Policy; and Reid Peyton Chambers, Partner at Sonosky, Chambers, Sachse, Endreson & Perry, LLP.

A highlight of the conference was the keynote address by the Honorable Randall R. Rader, Circuit Judge for the U.S. Court of Appeals For The Federal Circuit, who provided invaluable insights into the intersection of tribal law and the federal judiciary.

Dr. Alfred Balitzer, Chairman of the Board of the Foundation for California and a Member of the Board at Claremont Graduate University, underscored the significance of the event: "To have such an esteemed collection of minds converge to dissect and discuss the future of tribal sovereignty is extraordinary. This conference not only addressed the current state of affairs but also the far-reaching impact of federal policies and laws on Native American communities."

The event represented a rare and critical platform for thought leaders to discuss and shape the dialogue on tribal sovereignty, echoing a commitment to understanding and advocacy that continues to resonate through works like "The Native American Dream."

This narrative is about resilience, community, and forging alliances. Through exhaustive public dialogues, shifting policies, and pivotal legal changes, the tribes navigated this new frontier with keen eyes and determined hearts. The real threat of closure of their casinos by the U.S. Attorneys was their rallying point. Tribal leaders stood firm, traversing from San Diego to San Francisco, making compelling cases for the significance of tribal gaming. Beyond just persuasion, they showcased the sacred essence of their mission, marking an indelible commitment to their community's well-being and the high standards of their endeavors. Join us as we delve deeper in Chapter 1.

CHAPTER ONE

A Short Introduction to Indian Gaming

Indian gaming stands as a unique entity within the American capitalist economic system. Unlike any other business or industry, it explores pivotal questions regarding federal and tribal sovereignty. Its development has been significantly shaped by significant United States Supreme Court rulings, subject to Congressional statutes and hearings, impacted by major administrative decisions, and even addressed through presidential proclamations and executive orders. It's not private sector gaming akin to Las Vegas or other forms of gaming; it's distinctly tribal government gaming.

It is an industry that covers a very wide range of commercial activities, from simple bingo to the most advanced forms of electronic gaming. Some tribes in or near major metropolitan areas — the Mashantucket Pequots and the Mohegan Sun in Connecticut, the Florida Seminoles, and the San Manuel Band of Mission Indians in California — have achieved their initial economic goals. Today, they rival major corporations in terms of revenues, numbers of employees, and they have national, even international reputations. Most people do not know or understand that most tribal nations find themselves scraping by with an unpredictable existence given their remote locations.

No industry has changed more over the past three decades, and few continue to evolve in so many surprising ways. In the 1980s it would have been unthinkable that tribal gaming would generate $40 billion annually; that tribes would compete to attract 'casino tourism' and promote the 'casino experience' on their reservations; or that major investors (including the man who became the 45th president of the United States) would join their businesses. Today, some tribes have not only harnessed their gaming experience and expertise but have also ventured into owning and managing gaming operations in the heart of Las Vegas. This represents a testament to their growth, resilience, and entrepreneurial spirit.

Today, Indian gaming has developed its own constellation of service industries and associated professions. When we embarked on this journey over three decades ago, the landscape was sparse, with only a handful of attorneys possessing expertise in tribal and gaming law and a few tribal consultants such as Waltona Manion and Nicki Symington who were pioneers in the field. Today, the complexities of Indian law are covered in law school curricula, and top law firms compete to represent tribal interests. New professions have grown up catering to new tribal needs, including casino managers, tribal accountants, casino auditors, financial advisers, and even tribal health specialists. National and state lobbyists protect and promote tribal interests in legislative and regulatory processes. Top political consultants with experience in congressional or presidential campaigns advise tribal leaders on how to manage political problems. Public relations consultants help tribes with marketing and educational campaigns. And as a further remarkable development, increasing numbers of universities, colleges and business schools are now offering courses to students aspiring to join what they perceive to be one of the nation's growth industries.

The constitutional and historical background to the development of Indian gaming is explored in widely available publications. This chapter sets out only a few brief introductory notes on the major subjects, together with suggestions for further reading to give you background and a better understanding of the law and the challenges tribes face.

The United States Constitution and Congressional statutes set the stage for tribes across the nation. This book delves into the parallel stories of three tribes each striving to establish legalized gaming on their federally recognized reservations. Though they navigated the same regulatory landscape — shaped by milestone legal rulings, directives like the Indian Reorganization Act and the Indian Gaming Regulatory Act and supervised by pivotal federal agencies such as the Department of the Interior, the Bureau of Indian Affairs, and the National Indian Gaming Commission — each tribe's journey to their mutual objective was unique and diverse.

Despite operating within a uniform constitutional and legal landscape, these tribes carved out unique paths toward legalized gaming and self-reliance. The contrasts in their journeys are not merely chronological tales; they are deep dives into the multifaceted causes and challenges they encountered along the way. This book sheds light on both the commonalities and differences in their approaches, offering analytical insights into the complexities each tribe faced along the way.

Let's look at the foundational principles set by the U.S. Constitution and the influential Supreme Court cases that have shaped decision-making in this area.

Indians and the Constitution: Key Points. Article I, Section 2, Clause 3 and Article I, Section 8 of the Constitution refer to Indian Nations. The language has been interpreted as the basis of a unique federal-tribal relationship.

The role of tribes in the federal system was first spelled out in detail in three Supreme Court decisions, the so-called 'Marshall Trilogy:' *Johnson v. M'Intosh* in 1823, holding private citizens could not buy lands from Native Americans; *Cherokee Nation v. Georgia* in 1831, declaring the relationship of the Cherokee nation to the United States to be that of a "ward to its guardian;" and in 1832, *Worcester v. Georgia, which held* that only the federal government, not the states, could deal with Indian nations.

Over time, and with further judicial decisions and Congressional statutes, three basic principles developed governing Indian tribes. They may be stated quite simply as:

- **Trust relationship**: The federal government has a "duty to protect" the tribes.
- **Plenary power**: Congress has ultimate authority over Indian tribes.
- **Territorial sovereignty**: Indian tribes' rights to their land is 'organic,' not granted by the state in which they have a reservation; and they exercise sovereignty on that land, subject only to Congress.

Each of these case history chapters concludes with a section, 'Analysis,' covering the 'causal mechanisms' that were at work. The final chapter, Conclusions, draws upon these three case history analyses to compare the tribes across a number of subjects and circumstances. These include: the extent to which statutory intent and official policies determined outcomes; the role played by tribal sovereignty, especially when in conflict with community concerns; public opinion and attitudes, including racism; the role of informal powers and outside players; the role of investors in tribes' decisions; interactions with local, state and national agencies; the importance of tribal governing structures and policies, the roles of leaders; women in tribal leadership roles; tribal values and policy commitments; and politics within each tribe and between and among tribes.

Over the past three decades I have been collaborating with tribes, leveraging my expertise in public relations and marketing to tell their unknown stories. Even before the era of social media, we crafted campaigns that showcased the true essence of Indian gaming: the people, their rich history, and their aspirations. It was never just about slot machines; it's about a community's pursuit of self-reliance, self-governance, and a brighter future for generations ahead.

My insights into Indian gaming stem from my experience over the past three decades in the industry and various research initiatives I've led or overseen. Additionally, the relationships I've fostered with numerous tribes over the years have deeply influenced my perspective. I've wondered if my deep connections with tribal communities or my strongly held beliefs might influence my ability to objectively write this book. For instance, I firmly believe tribes have been subjected to double standards, where expectations, regulations, and treatments applied to them differ significantly from those applied to other non-tribal entities. This inconsistent approach, often stemming from federal, state, and local governments, has posed challenges and disparities for tribal communities in their pursuit of justice, rights, and opportunities.

With these questions in mind, I have made every effort to maintain objectivity and to present all relevant empirical evidence in their struggles to achieve self-reliance.

A Short History of Gaming on Indian Lands

Forced onto wilderness reservations by the federal government, Indian tribes consistently suffered the highest rates of poverty along with many other indicators of profound social and economic distress. At the end of the 19th century and extending well into the 20th century, federal policy towards the tribes was 'assimilationist:' in other words, to eliminate tribal culture in favor of incorporating Native Americans into mainstream society.

In the 1930s the so-called 'Indian New Deal' sought to restore tribal culture. The Indian Reorganization Act of 1934 returned some lands to the tribes and explicitly committed the United States to strengthen the traditional cultural and economic resources available to tribes.

Nevertheless, Indians were largely dependent on subsistence welfare and, in 1953, Congress passed Public Law 280, a major breach in the sovereign powers of tribal governments over their lands. The Act extended the criminal jurisdiction of six states (Alaska, California, Minnesota, Nebraska, Oregon, and Wisconsin) onto reservations.

Although few tribal reservations had any economic resources, Indian cultures had always practiced traditional games of chance. In the late 1970s and early 1980s, several tribes, led by those in Florida and California, opened bingo parlors to generate revenues and jobs on the reservation.

In 1979 the Florida Seminoles opened a high-stakes bingo hall. In the mid 1980's, California's Cabazon Band of Mission Indians and the Morongo Band of Mission Indians opened and ran bingo parlors with some card games. In 1986, the San Manuel Band of Mission Indians launched the nation's largest bingo hall and introduced machine games. At the same time, the Reagan administration, seeking to pare back welfare programs and emphasize 'self-sufficiency,' urged Congress to enact new policies for tribal gaming.

As the Cabazon and Morongo gaming operations grew, the State of California sought to close them down because they were seen as competitive with the state lottery. Led by their pre-eminent tribal attorney, Glenn Feldman, Cabazon filed a lawsuit, later joined by the Morongo Tribe suing California, claiming sovereign authority to operate gaming businesses on their own reservations. In 1987, the United States Supreme Court ruled for the Cabazon Band: with that decision, the stage was set for the expansion of Indian gaming, not only in California but nationwide.

In 1988, Congress passed, and President Ronald Reagan signed the Indian Gaming and Regulatory Act (IGRA). The legislation established that tribes could offer bingo and non-banked card games to the public so long as they adopted ordinances approved by a new federal agency, the National Indian Gaming Commission. Congress also established a regulatory scheme for casino-style gambling, known as Class III gaming, which included slot machines, craps, blackjack, and roulette. Such games could only be operated on two conditions: first, the games that the tribe wished to offer must already be lawfully permitted in the state; and second, the tribe must negotiate a compact, or an agreement, with the state for final approval by the Secretary of the Interior and the Bureau of Indian Affairs (BIA).

Federal Bureaucracy and Tribes

The Department of the Interior is responsible for the administration of programs relating to Native Americans as well as the management and conservation of most federal lands. In March 2021 Deb Haaland was appointed its Secretary, the first Native American to head the Department in its 170-year history.

IGRA established the National Indian Gaming Commission and mandated it to "support and promote tribal economic development, self-sufficiency, and strong tribal governments" through the operation of gaming on Indian lands. At least two members of the three-member Commission must be members of tribes.

The agency with which tribes have most contact is the Bureau of Indian Affairs (BIA). Perhaps no office in the Government of the United States has had a longer and more checkered history than this bureau, first formed to "protect domestic, dependent nations." In the first part of the 19th century, during the nation's westward expansion, the BIA was involved in the removal of the tribes from ancestral lands. Then in 1887 the Dawes Act forced the subdivision of tribal landholdings into allotments for Native American family heads and individuals, converting traditional systems of land tenure into private property. At the end of the 19th century and up until the early 1930s, it supervised the so-called cultural assimilation of the tribes and the education (or re-education) of their children (often by separation from their parents).

In the New Deal with the passage of the Indian Reorganization Act in 1934, the Bureau, under reforming Director John Collier, became responsible for reversing the assimilation policy and restoring some lost lands to the tribes. By the end of the 1960s and up through the 1970s, it confronted a surging tide of American Indian protests and civil rights demonstrations. In this period the BIA came under attack for using inconsistent procedures to deny or to recognize aboriginal titles. In 1975 the Indian Self-Determination and Education Act partially restored the traditional relationship between tribal lands and self-government; and in 1978 the BIA published standard criteria for federal recognition in the Federal Register.

After IGRA in 1988 was passed by a bi-partisan vote and signed into law by President Ronald Reagan, the BIA became central to decisions on land into trust and tribal-state compacts. Today, the BIA website declares its mission to be to "enhance the quality of life, to promote economic opportunity, and to carry out the responsibility to protect and improve the trust assets" of the tribes. The irony of the emphasis on its trust responsibilities is that it became clear in the 1990s that the BIA's gross mishandling of trust revenues had cost the tribes many billions of dollars, decades of poverty and the loss of millions, if not billions, of dollars of potential income.

IGRA, the basic federal statutory framework under which tribal casinos operate, has been the target of litigation in many states. Nowhere has it generated more lawsuits than in California. And in no other state have tribes had to deal with more political obstacles. In the next chapter, we will need to look closely at the development of Indian gaming in the Golden State.

California Gaming Politics: Balancing Rights and Realities

Research indicated that while many Californians were wary of local gambling, they overwhelmingly championed tribal self-reliance, leading to support for reservation-based tribal gaming.

For the Governor, these compacts represented not just potential revenue streams but a political tightrope. On one hand, negotiating a tough deal with a tribe could augment the state's coffers, benefiting Californians. There was a sizable portion of the electorate staunchly against gambling, and in certain areas, endorsing a casino could be politically detrimental.

State legislators were particularly attuned to these political undercurrents. Even among those who voted for Proposition 1A, there was a sentiment of 'Not in my backyard.' The legislators recognized the potential for their casino endorsements to become ammunition for electoral opponents.

The tribes, on their end, faced the delicate task of juxtaposing their inherent rights to self-governance and their quest for economic autonomy against a backdrop of 120 state legislators and the overarching California administration. Strategic messaging was essential, emphasizing the distinctions between tribal gaming and its corporate counterparts. Utilizing survey research, this communication strategy played a pivotal role in garnering the support of nearly two-thirds of the electorate for tribal gaming.

Intricacies of tribal politics permeated each phase. Tribes with operational casinos often resisted proposals by neighboring tribes, viewing them as competition. They exerted influence over the Governor and State Legislature, leveraging their new-found economic prowess. Over time, certain tribes, fortified by their gaming revenues, became significant contributors to legislative campaigns. This shift in the financial landscape meant that tribes became dominant campaign financiers in California. Some tribal leaders even emerged as formidable forces in state politics. Recognizing the need for solidarity and advocacy, California and Nevada tribes established the California Nevada Indian Gaming Association (CNIGA) in 1988, later to be renamed the California Nations Indian Gaming Association, dedicated to educational initiatives and safeguarding Indian gaming rights on recognized tribal reservations.

THE THREE TRIBES IN CALIFORNIA

CHAPTER TWO

The California Experience

In the diverse and complex history of California, tribes have weathered trials much like a sturdy oak tree enduring centuries of storms. Their journey, marked by shadows of oppression and loss, stands as a testament to the resilience of the human spirit. Just as an oak's roots run deep and unwavering, so do the roots of California's indigenous communities, firmly anchored in their ancestral lands.

In this chapter, we delve into the story of how California's tribes confronted seemingly insurmountable barriers, akin to formidable boulders in their path, fought back and ingeniously crafted solutions to advance towards self-reliance. Their struggles and triumphs offer profound insights into the invincible nature of the human will when driven by the pursuit of justice, equity, and self-determination.

California's tribes suffered many of the same tragedies as the other indigenous peoples of the Americas. Like others, they were victims of a centuries-long pandemic, one of the deadliest in human history: smallpox and other diseases brought by Europeans killed the greater part of the native population. This was only the first of the horrors that followed the arrival of white men.

California's 21 Spanish missions were an imperial project, directed from Madrid and endorsed by the highest authorities of the Roman Catholic church. Native American labor, slaves under the discipline of the Spanish whip, built the missions; Spanish military violence kept the tribes in subjection; and Spanish bigotry forced them to give up their language, culture, and religious beliefs. In many instances the women were subject to forced sterilization to exterminate the native population. As the missions grew, California's native population of Indians sharply declined.

California's tribes suffered more than other tribes under Spanish rule and more than other tribes when the United States displaced Mexican authority. In 1849 the tribes found themselves the target of a new master race, the Anglo-Americans. Flooding into California, lusting for gold and land, the new white men went on years-long killing sprees. Merely eight months after California's inclusion in the federal Union, the state legislature, on April 19, 1850, approved chilling legislation. Sanctioned by California's first Governor, Peter Hardeman Burnett, mere days later, the law brazenly advocated for the extermination of Indian populations, with government bounties routinely being issued for Indian scalps. California's new 'rule of law,' entitled "Act for the Government and Protection of Indians," nicknamed the "Indian Indenture Act," permitted bondage of Indian men and women; sale of their children into menial service was common; a tribal member arrested for drunkenness or loitering could be sold to the highest bidder; and no white man could be convicted of any crime, even murder, on the testimony of an Indian. The act facilitated the removal and displacement of Native Californians Indians from their traditional lands, separating at least a generation of children and adults from their families, languages, and cultures from 1850 to 1865.

Assemblymember James Ramos, a member of the San Manuel Band of Mission Indians, emphasized, "This is a crucial chapter in our history, as well as in the history of California and the American West, one that demands understanding and appreciation from everyone."

In contrast to the tribes in Alaska, Canada, and Mexico, California's native communities faced far greater losses. Their population declined significantly, and a substantial portion of their extensive land base was seized without compensation. As their numbers dwindled, even more of their tribal lands were seized, and they were forced ever further away into desert and wilderness territories, the lands deemed undesirable by others. Although the sufferings of tribes on the East coast and in the Mid-West are much better known, California's tribes were more thoroughly subjugated, lost more of their cultural heritage, and experienced more wholesale expropriation.

History and Opinion

Most late 20th-century white Californians were unaware of this dark chapter in their state's history. It wasn't until 1851, during California's inaugural State of the State Address, that the existence of California's tribes was officially recognized. Tragically, as we have shown above, California's first Governor, Peter Burnett signed legislation that facilitated the enslavement and subsequent genocide of Native Californians.

The first formal recognition and acknowledgment of the contributions from Native Americans in California came over a century later in 1968 when then Governor Ronald Reagan signed a resolution calling for the fourth Friday of September to be American Indian Day. Long overdue, this was merely a symbolic recognition of California Indians and achieved no improvement of tribal lives. It was not until 1998, a generation later, after a push from James Ramos and the San Manuel Band of Mission Indians, that the State of California began the process to begin teaching local California native history in classrooms.

For most Californians, even today, what they think they know about Indians is what they learned from Hollywood's 'cowboy' movies. None of California's other minorities experienced such a brutal centuries-long experience, but few Californians know even its basic facts. School children learn of the horrors of African American slavery, of the holocaust, and of the Japanese internment; but they are never told that California's first state government paid for the deliberate slaughter of Indians.

By contrast, California's tribal leaders know their history well. When they met opposition from government officials or were faced with hostile local opinion, they drew on the lessons they had learned from that history and their ancestors. Understandably, many Native Americans believed they still confront the age-old racism of white society.

Ignorant of the history, many non-Indians struggle to understand why Native Americans have special treatment under laws establishing an Indian 'monopoly' of gaming. Why were Indians not content with the same freedoms as other citizens? Why should 21st century white Californians, most of whose ancestors were not implicated in past horrors, be forced to put up with the social and cultural disturbances threatened by tribal gaming?

The California Constitution and Initiatives

The problem for California tribes wishing to offer casino-style games was that the games were not permitted under the state constitution: indeed, there was constitutional language that seemed explicitly to prohibit such games.

In 1996, several tribes were threatened with closure of their casinos: both federal and state authorities including the U.S. Marshals Service, condemned the casinos as illegal under the California constitution. To ensure the survival of their gaming casinos, the tribes had to instigate a change in state law to permit Vegas-style gaming. This eventually led to an effort that changed the state constitution. This endeavor to bring the matter before the people of California provided a temporary respite against federal and state moves to shutter their casinos.

Under the leadership of the San Manuel Band of Mission Indians, public opinion research was conducted that showed that the people of California would support tribal gaming on reservations if it was linked to helping tribes achieve economic independence and self-reliance. Following this research, the San Manuel tribe began an effort to organize all the California tribes and they contributed most of the money to qualify an initiative to change the law with Proposition 5. In 1998, after what was then the most expensive initiative campaign in state history, more than five million Californians supported Proposition 5 with 62.38% of the vote. The fact is more people voted for Proposition 5 than voted for Gray Davis for Governor.

The victory was short lived: Proposition 5 was deemed illegal by the California Supreme Court because it failed to change the language of the constitution. To keep their casinos open, the tribes had to campaign all over again in a new statewide election campaign. In 2000, again with a clear majority vote, the public passed Proposition 1A. This time, as a constitutional amendment, the initiative changed the state constitution to allow Class III gaming in the state.

Indian gaming would allow Indian self-reliance. Survey research showed us that this was the political message that permitted easy passage of both Propositions 5 and 1A. Big majorities of voters in all parts of the state approved the concept of assuring tribes' economic independence through tribal gaming operations on recognized reservations.

In addition to being legally permissible at the state level, a federal law, specifically the Indian Gaming Regulatory Act (IGRA), mandates that every federally recognized tribe seeking to operate a gaming facility must have a tribal-state compact. In September 1999, the California Governor and 57 tribes negotiated, and the legislature approved, the first tribal-state compacts for Class III gaming operations. These permitted tribes to conduct and operate slot machines, lottery games and banked and percentage card games on Indian land; but they also stipulated that a very significant share of revenues from the gaming operations would go to the state budget and another portion to the specific benefit of non-gaming tribes in the state.

Problems and Solutions

To some it now appeared that the California tribes had won a great and final victory. After all, they had proved in two statewide elections that sizeable majorities of the state's voters supported tribal gaming;

and their lawyers were assuring them that they could now operate casinos in full compliance with federal and state law.

Yet, for many California tribes, victory continued to be elusive and self-reliance far out of reach. Many obstacles still stood in their way — obstacles that tribes everywhere continue to face. In the following chapters, we will describe how three very different tribes faced those obstacles and the strategies that they deployed to overcome the odds to achieve self-reliance.

CHAPTER THREE

The San Manuel Band of Mission Indians

Over the last three decades, my firm has guided and helped to produce and air dozens of culturally rich and politically relevant television and radio commercials to promote public understanding of Tribal nations, sovereignty, and contemporary issues faced by Native Americans and tribal governments. We've created outreach programs, built coalitions, bolstered community management, pioneered a Tribal Certificate program for managers, instituted tribal investment funds, and established a tribal health concierge program dedicated to helping tribal families receive the best medical care possible.

San Manuel's only revenue-producing business at the time was a Bingo Hall that doubled as an entertainment venue during the evenings. Some nights would be standing room only, other nights the place was empty. Following my cold call to the tribe I sat down with tribal member and General Manager Ken Ramirez, and the marketing team led by Ted Dorney and Joe Bour. One of my first contracts was to conduct a market study of the Inland Empire and survey customers to ascertain what types of entertainment and which entertainers would draw the biggest audiences to San Manuel. Before we could conduct the study, we were asked to help the tribe plan meetings and events. This led to assisting the tribe in building community coalitions and support, and establishing relations with local, state, and federal governments.

My contacts with the San Manuel have not only been about business. Over three decades, friendships with the tribal citizens of San Manuel have been an important part of my life.

Our most important effort took place in 1997, when my company conducted a landmark survey that for the first time showed the people of California would in fact support Indian gaming. It was this survey that became the foundation and road map for two statewide ballot measures that would follow that ultimately changed the California constitution and legalized Indian gaming in the state. This launched San Manuel and other tribes in California on the road to self-reliance. Those who could open casinos now could do it legally and those who were not able to open casinos would also benefit from Indian gaming. It should be noted that not all tribes chose to go into gaming: and for some like the Yurok Tribe, which had a growing economy and opportunities for their tribal members, initially decided not to go into gaming.

At a crucial juncture in time, armed with the survey findings, the San Manuel Business Committee convened upstairs in the bingo hall meeting rooms. Here, they engaged in discussions with Senator Richard Polanco and Assemblyman Tony Cardenas regarding potential strategies with the California legislature and the broader public. In the face of widespread skepticism, Ken Ramirez expressed unwavering belief in the feasibility of their goals, emphasizing that with the right individuals and backing, anything is achievable.

To help set the stage for this case history, I set out below some facts on the major participants.

The Tribe

The area occupied by the San Manuel Band of Mission Indians was historically inhabited by the Serrano Indians. The name Serrano, given by the Spanish Conquistadores and Mission Friars, was applied to highland people who were subdued by the Mission Friars from which the name Mission Indians derives.

SAN MANUEL
BAND OF MISSION INDIANS

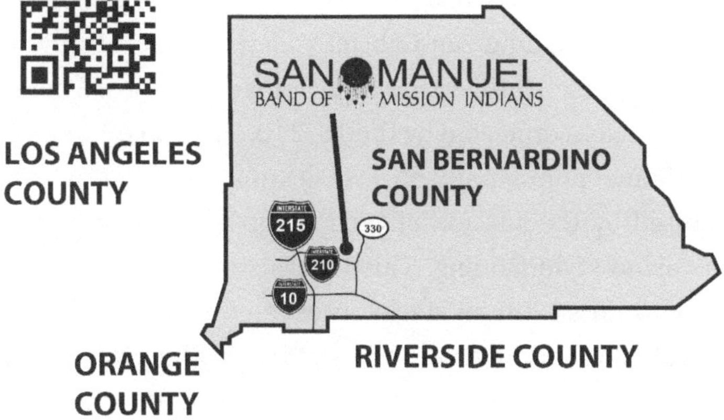

The San Manuel Band are members of the Yuhaaviatam clan, indigenous to the San Bernardino mountains and steep foothills bordering the San Bernardino Valley. The Band and the reservation were named after Santos Manuel, a great tribal leader who in 1866 led his people into the mountains of San Bernardino away from local white militias who had tried to exterminate them and drive them from lands they had lived on for centuries. Santos Manuel was still their leader in the in the early days of the reservation which was established in 1891.

The U.S. Government officially recognized the tribe in 1891 and granted them 657 acres of land in the San Bernardino mountains. This area was later expanded to 900 acres, and the tribe has been actively purchasing additional land to expand their reservation ever since. Only three acres of the original reservation were flat or arable, sufficient for agriculture, or suitable for any form of economic development. On the flat three acres, the tribe planted an apricot orchard, which for decades was the tribe's only source of income. Selling apricots outside of the reservation produced little revenue and most tribal members were forced to leave for employment elsewhere.

In the mid-1980s, inspired by the success of bingo games run by the Seminole tribe in Florida and a few Californian tribes, San Manuel chose to launch a high-stakes bingo hall. Its success wasn't just due to its closeness to Highland and San Bernardino. It benefited greatly from being near the bustling San Gabriel Valley, a stone's throw from Los Angeles and close to Riverside and Orange Counties. These densely populated areas, connected by the 10, 210, 215 and 60 freeways, making San Manuel popular and an easy destination to get to.

Inspired by the success of their bingo hall, the tribe planned to launch casino style gaming. This case history chronicles their early struggles to do so, the obstacles presented to this ambition by the state, local and federal governments, their leading role in campaigns for statewide initiatives to legalize Indian gaming, and finally their emergence as the largest employer in the area and a recognized economic powerhouse in California.

At that time, the Business Committee was comprised of the following elected members: Chairman Henry Duro, Vice-Chairman Ken Ramirez, and Tribal Councilmembers James Ramos, Jamie Guerrero, and Audrey Martinez.

The County and Two Cities

San Bernardino County, 80% of which is federally owned land, is geographically the largest county in the United States, covering an area from the 10 freeway to the Nevada border and the Colorado River. The bulk of the population lives in two areas: one is south of the San Bernardino Mountains and adjacent to Riverside; and the other is composed of the cities of San Bernardino and Highland.

In 1980, the County had a population of 900,000, a figure that grew to 1,400,000 in 1990 and to 2,100,000 in 2010, making it one of the fastest growth areas in the nation. The surge in numbers was driven by rapidly rising home prices in Los Angeles County and by the arrival of large numbers of Latino residents. By 2010, the Latino population had risen to half of the County's total.

The County is divided between heavily Latino and mostly Democratic areas and more affluent, largely white, and mostly Republican areas. The result is that candidates from both major political parties have won in recent elections. Thus, the heavily Latino city of Ontario votes Democrat, but traditionally with very low turnout, while the more affluent city of Redlands has high turnout and votes Republican. Over the past three decades, the County has been troubled by corruption, high crime rates, insolvency, and lack of housing — issues that have been showcased in local and national media.

Two cities in the County — Highland and the City of San Bernardino — are important to this case history. Both fall well below California's median family income levels, both experienced explosive growth in the 1980s and 1990s, both saw rapid increases in their Latino population, and both were troubled by growing crime rates. The closure of Norton Air Force Base in 1994, caused a loss of more than 15,000 jobs and $4 billion loss to the annual economy, adding to their economic difficulties and causing deep budgetary problems; but it was San Bernardino that fell into bankruptcy.

San Manuel's reservation includes portions of the cities of San Bernardino and Highland and unincorporated areas of the County.

Two Governors

In the period from the mid-1960s through the first decades of the new century, California's governors tended to alternate between Democrat and Republican, liberal and conservative. Pat Brown, a liberal Democrat, was defeated for re-election by Ronald Reagan, who in turn was succeeded by Pat Brown's son, Jerry. Then, two Republicans, George Deukmejian, and Pete Wilson, were followed in office by liberal Democrat Gray Davis who was recalled and succeeded by Republican Arnold Schwarzenegger. Jerry Brown then reappeared for a second two-year term and was followed by fellow Democrat Gavin Newsom.

This case history, although its roots stretch back into the 1960s and the narrative continues into recent years, focuses on the policies and actions of two of these California Governors: the 36th, Pete Wilson (1991-99), and the 37th, Gray Davis (1999-2003).

Wilson (born 1933), a Yale graduate, a Marine Corps officer, and an attorney with a degree from Boalt Hall, won election to the California State Assembly in 1966. He then became a popular, three-term Mayor of San Diego until 1983, when he was elected to the United States Senate. He resigned from the Senate after winning the 1990 California gubernatorial election. It's important to note that Governor Wilson was opposed to all gaming in California, especially gaming that he believed was outside of what was legal in the state's constitution.

Although a moderate on social issues, Wilson was governor during the Los Angeles Riots of 1992 and developed a reputation at that time for being 'tough on crime.' As governor, he signed a three-strikes law and supported re-imposition of the death penalty. He also advocated passage of California Proposition 187 which, until struck down in federal courts, would have prevented illegal immigrants from receiving social services. Wilson was ambitious to be President and sought the nomination of his party in 1996, losing to Bob Dole.

Joseph Graham "Gray" Davis Jr. (born 1942), a Stanford Graduate with a JD from Columbia, was a Vietnam veteran awarded the Bronze Star, who had a long career in California politics. He was chief of staff to Governor Jerry Brown (1975–81), a California State Assemblyman (1983–87), California State Controller (1987–95) and Lieutenant Governor (1995–99).

Davis won the 1998 general election for governor with 58% of the vote, portraying himself as a moderate centrist Democrat who would end Pete Wilson's "divisive politics." He was easily re-elected in 2002. Only a few months into his second term, however, he became the first California governor to be recalled. He was widely blamed for spending too much time on fundraising in a period when California's politics were roiled by the energy crisis and the dot com bubble. Tribal contributions made up a significant part of Davis' campaign funds.

Wilson and Davis pursued widely differing policies on tribal gaming and their actions produced markedly different results for San Manuel and the California tribes.

The Hotel Employees and Restaurant Employees Union

This labor union, known by its acronym HERE, was founded in the late 19th century, affiliating with the AFL-CIO in the mid-20th century. It gained public recognition and notoriety when it organized the staff of Yale University in 1984. Among major employers that contracted with this union were large casinos, Harrah's, Caesars Palace and Wynn Resorts and major hotel chains like Hilton, Hyatt (except in Sacramento) and Starwood.

In 1986, HERE was cited by the President's Commission on Organized Crime as being controlled by mob elements. Over the succeeding decade it was investigated by the U.S. Justice Department's Organized Crime and Racketeering Section. In 1995, HERE was forced into a compliance agreement with the U.S. Department of Labor to sever its ties with organized crime.

The federal civil racketeering complaint alleged that between 1970 and 1995, "the general executive board of the union cooperated with organized crime in soliciting bribes from employers, stealing union funds and denying union members the right of honest service by their officials." That settlement followed an earlier civil racketeering case against HERE's Local 54, involving casinos in Atlantic City.

The case history will explore HERE's tactics in attempting to force unionization on San Manuel's casino and other tribal gaming operations in California.

The Case History

Early in the Twentieth century, the Progressives outlawed gambling in Nevada, and it was not until 1931 that it was again legalized. Ever since, Californians have made the easy drive from Los Angeles to Las Vegas (less than four hours by the I-15 freeway). We will show how San Manuel's reservation, located close to the I-15 freeway, became a principal rival in California of the Vegas Strip.

The Birth of a Gaming Powerhouse: San Manuel's Bingo Revolution

As briefly noted above, the tribe's development as a major gaming power began modestly in 1986 when they opened a facility offering bingo, a game that was legal in California, employed by many churches as a fund-raising vehicle, and often played in many church halls across the state. As such, bingo was a respectable, low stakes form of gambling. Sometimes, other groups, again mostly charities and some fraternal organizations, might make their bingo more interesting by raising the jackpot in a 'cover all' game or permitting a progressive jackpot to increase until a final victor emerged. While bingo didn't carry the thrill and risk of high-stakes casino games, many saw it more as entertainment, often associated with churches and non-profits, rather than gambling.

East coast casinos developed high stakes variations on bingo, some giving an experience akin to playing on a video slot machine, others providing a rough equivalent to casino table games. Then in the late 1970s and early 1980s, the Seminole tribe, headquartered at their Hollywood reservation in Florida, began to launch their own high stakes version of bingo.

In the 1980s, the Morongo and Cabazon tribes, neighbors of the San Manuel tribe to the east, down the 10 freeway, had also started bingo halls to emulate the success of the Seminoles; but their facilities were smaller than that at San Manuel. In early 1987, when the Supreme Court's *Cabazon* ruling held that California could not forbid bingo and poker on tribal reservations, San Manuel was set to match the Seminoles in a very big way.

San Manuel's Chairman, Henry Duro, the Vice-Chairman Ken Ramirez, Audrey Martinez, Jamie Barron and James Ramos realized that a large-scale bingo operation could help with the ongoing economic challenges the tribe faced. Eager to open a successful operation and trying not to reinvent the wheel, San Manuel recruited and paid members of the Seminole's management team in Florida not only to provide skilled guidance but to remain in California and help establish and run the bingo operation.

On July 21, 1986, the San Manuel Indian Bingo opened its doors for business. Their success in a new 100,000 square foot bingo hall was achieved not only with bingo tables but with other gaming opportunities as well. There were 3,000 seats for players in what was the largest bingo hall in the country at the time. With such a large entertainment venue, the tribe became more and more interested in increasing their customer base by providing major entertainment.

By 1995, the profits from bingo were beginning to change the character of the San Manuel reservation and to improve the lives of tribal members. The giant facility was employing several hundred people, including tribal members who had previously depended on jobs paying minimum wages. Those who had been dependent on public assistance now came off welfare. The tribe began to provide some basic health services that had formerly been lacking and paid small monthly stipends to all tribal members.

Norris and Seagal Ignite an Initiative for Indian Self-Reliance

Bingo funded the next stage of San Manuel's road to self-reliance. The tribe had already deployed a few slot machines of the kind that had long been used in Nevada casinos. Then in 1995-6, they used their bingo revenues to bring in many such machines in an area that then began to expand at the expense of bingo. Soon, the slots were attracting customers both long before and then after the bingo games.

Each day, a multitude of patrons, primarily comprising retirees, eagerly fed their coins into the newly introduced machines, creating an atmosphere tinged with the scent of cigarette smoke. On weekends, the influx of customers extended beyond local communities, drawing visitors from across the expansive Greater Los Angeles metropolitan region. San Manuel pioneered an expansive and highly effective bussing initiative, attracting visitors from as far as San Diego and Las Vegas. Many of these patrons were individuals who had traditionally journeyed to Las Vegas for their gaming entertainment.

The profits from the slots soon began to dwarf the revenues from bingo. Other tribes saw this and, to emulate San Manuel, bought or leased their own slot machines. They did so with the belief that the *Cabazon* decision and the Indian Gaming Regulatory Act protected them legally.

Governor Pete Wilson pointed out that California law prohibited Vegas-style gaming against the house, and permitted only gaming against other players, and on that basis declared the machines illegal. Since IGRA limited tribes to the kinds of gaming permitted under state law, the federal government joined in declaring the slots illegal. Joined by other California tribes with slots, San Manuel took its stand on their claim to tribal sovereignty and their right to use their reservations as they choose. In response, the State government urged county sheriffs to close the tribal facilities and, in early 1996, the federal government sent in U.S. Attorneys to force tribal governments to close their casinos. State and federal authorities declared a willingness to use all necessary force to close what they saw as illegal gaming facilities.

Under pressure to close their casinos, the tribes held a series of meetings to discuss possible options with US Attorney Nora Manella and US District Judge Spencer Letts. The judge was clear: because casino gaming in California was not legal, the only option for all tribes was to shut down their casinos immediately.

Having had a small taste of success, the few tribes that were operating casinos bonded together to fight the federal and state government.

Within 72 hours I joined Waltona Manion and other consultants and the tribes from TASIN, the Tribal Alliance of Sovereign Indian Nations, to organize a political rally on the steps of the U.S. Courthouse in downtown Los Angeles. In a bold and historic decision, Tribal leaders stood ready to face incarceration to safeguard their casinos, showing unwavering commitment to keep them operational. Uniting in solidarity, TASIN Chairwoman Lynn Valbuena (San Manuel), Chairman Henry Duro (San Manuel), Ken Ramirez (San Manuel), Mary Ann Andreas (Morongo), Bobby Salgado (Soboba), Richard Milanovich (Agua Caliente), Mark Macarro (Pechanga), Rosemary Salgado (Soboba), Vincent Armenta (Santa Ynez), Michelle Salgado (Cahuilla), John James (Cabazon), Brenda Soulliere (Cabazon), Chairman Dean Mike (29 Palms) and Mary Belardo (Torres Martinez) gathered on the steps of the federal courthouse, waving signs, rallying a large crowd that clogged the streets of Los Angeles to express their support for Indian gaming in California.

TASIN TRIBES

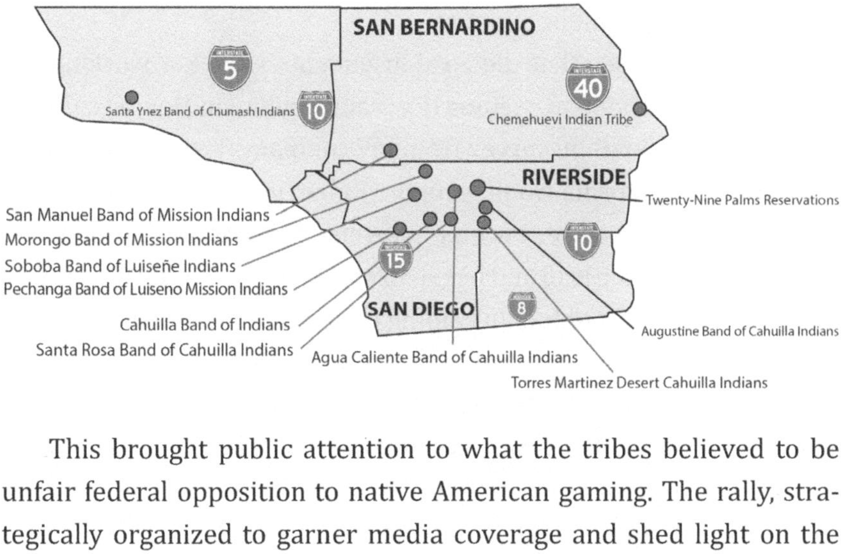

This brought public attention to what the tribes believed to be unfair federal opposition to native American gaming. The rally, strategically organized to garner media coverage and shed light on the federal government's attempts to shutter tribal casinos, achieved remarkable success. It sent a powerful message as it effectively brought downtown Los Angeles to a standstill, with an impressive turnout of over 3,000 individuals united in passionately demonstrating their steadfast support for Indian gaming and the relentless pursuit of tribal self-reliance in California. Chairwoman Lynn Valbuena emphasized, "Closing our casino doors was not an option. We had come too far and had no alternative but to stand united, defending our sovereignty and our fundamental right to self-reliance."

On May 5, 1997, tribes met with US District Judge Spencer Letts about the order to shut down their casinos. The tribal attorneys continued to argue that the federal government lacked the authority to close the casinos because the tribes were sovereign independent governments. The Judge, not convinced by the tribe's arguments, told the tribes in no uncertain terms to close their casinos immediately.

Of the 40 or so California tribes that were operating gambling casinos a group of nine insisted that they would keep their casinos open. They even brought in bull dozers and other equipment to block roads to keep sheriffs and US Attorneys off their reservations. The threat of a violent standoff with the authorities began to loom, for the first-time losing tribes their public support.

Beginning to see that the legal arguments were not working and looking for any option to keeping the casino open, San Manuel commissioned a public opinion survey from my company. The survey showed the voters of California would support Indian gaming when viewed as a means of helping tribes become self-reliant. It was at this point, that San Manuel took the lead and began to make a major shift in their strategy to secure legalized Indian gaming under California law.

Based on the survey research, and after a careful review of options, San Manuel decided to ask the public to show support for Indian gaming to stave off the U.S. Attorneys and the threatened closure of their gaming facility. In a move designed to capture attention and engagement, when the imminent closure of the casinos became a pressing issue, San Manuel swiftly took its message directly to the people of California. They enlisted the support of Chuck Norris, a highly recognizable actor with a popular television show at the time, to star in a statewide television commercial. Norris, celebrated for his roles as a champion against injustice and defender of the underdog, brought with him a formidable reputation that amplified the tribe's cause.

My company along with Mark and Sidney Galanty produced the 30-second television commercial in which Norris asked the people of California to support tribal self-reliance through reservation gaming. He made the case that the federal government was unfairly trying to close tribal gaming and he asked the people of California to step in, stop federal intervention and support Indian self-reliance.

At the close of the commercial, Norris asked Californians to show their support by calling an 800 number to express their support for tribal self-reliance. Those who called left their names, phone numbers and addresses for future campaign support. The Norris commercial ran on statewide television and was seen by more than 20 million people over a three-week period.

As a crucial part of their comprehensive strategy, immediately following the Norris commercial, San Manuel engaged Steven Seagal, another renowned celebrity celebrated for his roles in crime-fighting and confronting 'villains.' Collaborating with Galanty & Company, a premier media, branding and strategic firm in the nation, we produced a subsequent statewide TV commercial urging Californians to stand strong for tribal self-reliance. The same 800 number was used to expand a growing support database, and the commercial ran statewide for three weeks, reaching almost 25 million people.

Over six weeks, these commercials amassed a database of more than two million names from viewers who called the 800 number in support of tribal self-reliance in California. This formed the bedrock for two statewide campaigns, with self-reliance as the centerpiece, rallying the support of millions of Californians for this cause. The resounding backing of over 2 million people sent a potent message to both the federal government and the state of California: tribes were undeniably advancing towards legalizing gaming in the state.

Wilson and Schwarzenegger's Divide and Conquer Strategies

Meanwhile, Governor Wilson had set himself to divide the tribes and assert state control over Indian gaming. State law allowed gambling and games in which bettors played against each other, not against the house: that is, a player placed bets against other players for the pool of prize money created by all their bets.

Machines (known as Class II machines) to provide this type of play were brought into the state and a few California tribes were persuaded to deploy them. They were versions of Las Vegas slots but modified in several ways: they were operated by buttons, not levers, took in bills not coins, and paid out winnings with vouchers not cash. Essentially, they were high-speed electronic lottery games in which the casino kept a set fraction of the pot. Their advantage was that they were fully legal in California.

The new machines were first publicly unveiled and made available by the Pala Band of Mission Indians in northern San Diego County. Stan McGarr, Pala tribal secretary, speaking of the use of the new machines, told the San Francisco Chronicle, "The governor and the state have agreed to this. We can use this to get into gaming now, without any more legal problems." A few other tribes, attracted by the prospect of a truce with state and federal authorities, adopted 'Pala slots', including the Jackson Indian Rancheria some 400 miles north of San Manuel in Amador County.

State officials compared the Pala slots to a lottery scratcher game, a benign and popular form of gambling, with a predetermined number of winners. They warned against the corruption possible with 'Vegas slots' that permit casinos to control the payout.

San Manuel's leadership in communicating with other tribes emphasized the expense of the Pala slots, claimed they would be much less popular with their customers, and noted that their money-making potential was unclear. A concern, not so openly expressed, was that the state was insisting on strict limitations on the numbers of machines permitted to each tribe.

Governor Wilson's support of the Pala slots was only partially successful in dividing the gaming tribes. Most of the tribes refused to accept Pala machines and only a few tribes, who shared a common tribal attorney signed up for their use.

Empowering the People: Building Support for Tribal Gaming

San Manuel's leadership believed Governor Wilson was beyond persuasion. He had not only backed the Pala machines but had staked out a public position from which he could not back down. In 1996, I collaborated with the Foundation for California to organize a conference at Claremont McKenna College, focusing on the impacts of Indian Gaming. During this event, George Dunn, Chief of Staff to Governor Pete Wilson, unequivocally declared the Governor's unwavering stance against Indian gaming. He asserted that Governor Wilson would maintain his position, standing firm in opposition to Indian gaming, and was even prepared to take measures to close the casinos.

During the same conference, representatives of the federal government hinted at a potential shift in their perspective. They noted that in states where wagering against the house was allowed, East Coast tribes had successfully established Vegas-style casinos with full federal approval. Consequently, if California's gambling laws could be altered through the initiative process, federal authorities indicated that they might reconsider their opposition to Indian gaming in the state.

In early 1997, San Manuel conducted the first survey in the nation of voter opinion on Indian gaming which, as previously noted, showed that the people of California would in fact support tribal gaming. The only fact known from previous opinion polls for card clubs was that three of every four people in California were opposed to opening a card club in their neighborhood. Nevertheless, the bottom-line finding of the 1997 survey was that a big majority — 64% — of voters would support tribal gaming, so long as casinos were located on reservations. San Manuel decided that the only way to keep their casino open was to take this issue to the voters of California.

The survey research found that voters would favor Native Americans' rights to have limited gaming — but only so long as it was restricted to their tribal lands. Therefore, it was evident that voter outreach efforts needed to underscore the constraints of limited gaming on reservations. Additionally, the survey revealed that voters were receptive to the notion of advancing Indian self-reliance, reducing welfare dependence, and easing the burden on public finances. Consequently, the campaign's messaging had to prominently feature the concept of "tribal self-reliance," enabling Native Americans to attain economic independence.

Another crucial theme endorsed by the research was the significance of utilizing gaming revenues to assist non-gaming tribes and bolster their educational and healthcare initiatives, ensuring that all Native Americans could share in the benefits of tribal gaming.

The true question at hand was whether Californians would support such a measure. Although the survey results appeared favorable, it was clear that most residents possessed limited knowledge about tribes, tribal gaming, or the enduring challenges Native Americans had confronted, marked by deprivation and discrimination. Advocating for self-reliance through gaming necessitated demonstrating the tribes' pressing needs and the moral imperative of allowing them to pursue economic independence. Consequently, San Manuel opted to initiate an extensive public education campaign, unveiling the history of California's Native Americans to the local population for the first time, thus shedding light on their heritage and struggles.

San Manuel's objective was to establish a solid groundwork in public opinion for the upcoming campaign. Subsequently, the tribe believed it would be easier to enlist the support of other tribes who might have been skeptical about the potential success of the initiative process. This collaborative effort would be crucial in advancing the campaign.

Building a Tribal Coalition

While San Manuel was diligently forming a statewide coalition of tribal support, the tribe's leadership convened with election law attorneys to outline the essential components of an initiative measure. They reached a consensus on several critical aspects:

1. Allowing tribal casinos to install or retain Class III video-style slot machines, conduct lotteries, and host card games.

2. Mandating that the governor approve such gambling arrangements upon request from any tribe.

3. Requiring tribes with gambling operations to allocate a portion of their earnings to public interest funds and non-gaming tribes.

4. Entrusting tribes with primary responsibility for casino oversight, supplemented by some state regulation and oversight funded by the tribes.

San Manuel held a strong belief that Phase I, gaining support from fellow gaming tribes, would be a straightforward endeavor. After all, San Manuel had single-handedly financed the entire public education campaign up to this point, and it seemed reasonable to expect other gaming tribes to join a coalition in favor of an initiative measure.

I compiled and consolidated the survey results, along with evidence of the heightened public support resulting from the Norris and Seagal commercials and alongside San Manuel Vice Chairman Ken Ramirez, we set out on a journey to visit all 109 reservations in California, advocating for the notion of allowing the public to determine the future of Indian gaming. It appeared to be a relatively simple task at the outset. What could possibly go wrong?

To our astonishment, we encountered staunch opposition right from the start. The initial dozen tribes we approached firmly rejected our proposal. They expressed skepticism about Californians supporting Indian gaming and refused to invest their name or resources in such a campaign. Some tribes even brought in their consultants and lobbyists to bolster their arguments, vehemently insisting that we were pursuing an improbable dream and demanding that we immediately abandon the initiative. They made it abundantly clear that they believed our effort to let the people decide would undoubtedly fail and followed by asking us to immediately leave the reservation.

Undaunted by these discouraging reactions, we persisted in our outreach efforts. It wasn't until we met with the Pechanga Band of Luiseño Indians that we secured our first commitment to join a coalition of tribes. The Pechanga tribe dispatched several of its tribal members, including Butch Murphy, Patrick Murphy, and Anthony Miranda, to join the cause. They became part of the team as we crisscrossed the state, engaging with tribes about the prospect of joining the coalition to legalize Indian gaming. Chairman Mark Macarro, from the Pechanga Tribe, later emerged as the public face of our campaign.

After approximately two months of extensive travel throughout the state, personally visiting over 85 reservations, the tide began to turn. One by one, tribes decided to support our efforts. Even six out of the eleven tribes that had initially committed to the Pala machines opted to join our campaign. The turning point signaling a tribal consensus in favor of an initiative campaign came with the endorsements of the Tribal Alliance of Sovereign Indian Nations (TASIN) and the California Nations Indian Gaming Association (CNIGA). For the first time California's tribes united to garner support and win over the hearts and minds of voters.

Recognizing that most Californians lacked knowledge about the state's tribes, San Manuel initiated a comprehensive education effort to promote a better understanding of tribal sovereignty, history, culture, and tribal governance. This extensive program featured more than 50 distinct commercials across statewide television, radio, billboards, and newspapers, reaching hundreds of millions of people. Led by Vincent Duro and followed by San Manuel tribal members Melonie Calderon, Lynn Valbuena, Carla Rodriguez and James Ramos, these commercials marked a historic moment as tribal representatives took center stage to educate the public about the history, culture, and issues facing Native Americans in California. Alongside San Manuel tribal members, we reached out to renowned tribal advocates to join us in the mission of educating Californians about the critical challenges confronting Native Americans. Notably, former Assistant Secretary of the Interior for Indian Affairs, Kevin Gover, a well-known voice of reason and compassion, played a significant role in this enduring educational endeavor.

The ads covered a wide range of topics, from economic self-reliance to the unjust federal attempts to close tribal casinos, tribal sovereignty, and the dark history of oppression and land expropriation. Throughout Prop. 5, we collaborated with other tribal leaders such as Erica Pinto, Bill Mesa from Jamul, Vincent Armenta from Santa Ynez, and Duane and Alec Garfield from Tule River to ensure that the voices advocating for tribal self-reliance resonated with the people of California.

San Manuel, in collaboration with Jerry Levine and other attorneys, crafted the language for a ballot measure. As the federal government pressed for casino closures and established a shutdown date for all gaming operations, the majority of tribes rallied behind a campaign to qualify this measure for the ballot. The rationale behind this move was that if the measure could secure a spot on the ballot, the federal judge would likely acknowledge a genuine chance of legal reform and consequently delay the closures until the election outcomes were determined. Fingers crossed, we embarked on an expedited effort to sway opinions.

Phase I of the strategy targeted everyday Californians through a comprehensive public education initiative. This program was crafted to unveil the harsh truths, largely unfamiliar and uncomfortable for many non-Indians, regarding the atrocities perpetrated against Native American tribes, their enduring fight for survival on remote reservations, and how gaming had finally emerged as a pathway out of poverty, paving the way toward self-reliance.

Rev. Jesse Jackson and the Rainbow Coalition Champion Tribal Self-Reliance

In our relentless pursuit of support and unity, James Ramos, a dedicated member of the tribe's Business Committee, embarked on a mission that would forever alter our journey. He reached out to the renowned civil rights leader, Reverend Jesse Jackson, who not only accepted our cause but also brought with him the mighty force of the Rainbow Coalition.

"It was a pivotal moment, requiring a courageous leap across cultural boundaries in our quest for self-reliance. We understood that this endeavor transcended our immediate interests and enjoyed widespread support. Winning this battle would yield benefits for every community," articulated James Ramos.

Rev. Jackson's Rainbow Coalition was more than a symbol; it embodied his dream of uniting diverse communities, transcending racial and ethnic boundaries. It was an ambitious vision of unity.

In August 1997, under Rev. Jackson's leadership, the Rainbow Coalition joined tribal leaders and embarked on an epic journey across California, spanning from San Diego to Sacramento. This wasn't just symbolic support; it was a profound commitment to solidarity. Notably, this event coincided with the scorching heat of August, making it an even more formidable endeavor. We had to shield ourselves with sunscreen and constantly hydrate to endure the relentless sun.

San Manuel didn't stand idly by; it actively led this crusade by orchestrating a week-long bus tour with tribal leaders, led by influential figures like Jesse Jackson and Reverend Al Sharpton, flanked by Rainbow Coalition members. On the first day, our delegation, which included Chairman Henry Duro, Ken Ramirez, James Ramos, Priscilla Hunter (Chairwoman from Coyote Valley) and Polly Girvin (Coyote Valley Attorney) walked alongside Jackson, Sharpton, and around a hundred others who came out to show their support. Along the way, we would stop and talk to community members, local elected officials and business owners about the educational campaign. As we talked to more people, more of them supported Indian self-reliance. Each day, we embarked on a grueling ten-mile journey, symbolizing the resilience and determination of the tribes.

Wherever Jesse Jackson went, the media followed, and this event significantly contributed to gaining recognition and widespread support for tribal sovereignty across California. Headlines read: "Jackson, Sharpton Join Tribes in Sovereignty Walk."

This effort wasn't just about crossing ethnic boundaries; it marked the first time the African American community stood in unity with Native Americans, Asians, Hispanics, and others to champion tribal self-reliance. Though the days were physically demanding, they were equally rewarding. We learned the importance of proper footwear, but more profoundly, we understood the value of outreach, unity, and the resonance of shared visions that every community could rally behind.

Not This Time, HERE – A Clash of Wills with HERE Union: Tribes Defend Their Sovereignty

The Hotel Employees and Restaurant Employees Union (HERE) had a reputation for getting its way in the world of politics. Led by the formidable Political Director, Jack Gribbon, a relentless negotiator who never accepted defeat, the Union found itself facing an unexpected challenge when dealing with tribal interests.

Gribbon had a track record of targeting organizations that HERE aimed to unionize. His approach was straightforward: attend a meeting, lay out his demands to the owners, and typically walk away with an agreement. The Union, a significant contributor to legislative races, granted Gribbon considerable influence in Sacramento and a potent tool to wield when pushing owners to embrace unionization. The tribes proved to be a different kind of adversary, unlike any Gribbon had encountered in his career.

It all began in Sacramento, California, during a meeting of tribal leaders convened to discuss their compact negotiations. I was present at this gathering, bearing witness to the unfolding drama. An unexpected request reached the room, seeking permission for a certain Jack Gribbon to address the tribal leaders.

During a break, it was decided to allow him to speak, even though none of the leaders were familiar with his name. The moment Gribbon entered the room, he aimed to assert his dominance. He wasted no time in making it clear that it was his way or the highway, threatening to disrupt both the tribes and the ongoing tribal-state compacts negotiated with the Governor. What Gribbon didn't realize was that he had walked into a room filled with leaders who staunchly believed in tribal sovereignty and were unyielding in their commitment to making decisions independently.

As Gribbon began to speak, he loudly proclaimed his superiority, warning the tribes of impending hardships if they failed to comply with his demands. After enduring his tirade for about 20 minutes, he was promptly shown the door and deemed unwelcome on California reservations.

This decision infuriated Gribbon, who promptly attempted to wield his political influence in the state capital to obstruct the tribes during their compact negotiations. Members of the legislature rejected his approach for perhaps the first time in his career. He was met with resistance from political leaders, who instructed him to step aside and refrain from interfering with the compacts. He was further informed that if he sought to unionize Indian casinos, he would need to negotiate individually with each casino. Unaccustomed to such opposition, Gribbon and HERE responded with threats and intimidation aimed at both tribes and casino employees. Yet, the tribes stood their ground.

HERE's efforts to unionize were consistently rebuffed by tribe after tribe until they finally resorted to filing a lawsuit against San Manuel. This lawsuit prompted Congress to reevaluate the National Labor Relations Act of 1935 and consider exemptions for casinos and other tribal enterprises from this law.

In the end, the tribes agreed to allow HERE onto their reservations to attempt to organize hotel and restaurant employees. This saga taught valuable lessons. HERE recognized its limitations in trying to force tribes into unionization, while tribes saw the political and human resources advantages of affording certain classifications of workers the opportunity to organize if they so desired.

Qualifying the Measure – A Race Against Time to Stave Off Closure

As the federal deadline for casino closures loomed just thirty days away, the tribes embarked on a monumental task: collecting signatures to place the measure on the ballot for the upcoming November election. But how many signatures were needed to meet this crucial requirement?

In California, the number of signatures required to secure a spot on the ballot hinges on the total number of votes cast for the governor in the preceding election. In 1994, this total had reached a staggering 8,665,000 votes. To qualify a citizen-initiated amendment to the California Constitution, a daunting 8 percent of that total was needed, translating to 693,230 signatures. For an initiated statute, 5 percent of the votes cast for the governor, equivalent to 433,269 signatures, were required. Qualifying a statutory measure seemed more manageable, but given the extraordinary time constraints, it posed a colossal, costly, and potentially insurmountable challenge that had never been done before.

In California, individuals who sign a petition for a citizen-initiated measure must be registered voters. Specialized initiative drive firms excel at collecting such signatures, often charging several dollars for each valid signature. These firms understand that a significant percentage of the signatures they gather will be disqualified due to various issues, such as the signer's name not appearing on the electoral roll of registered voters, signature mismatches, missing addresses, or other faults. Further complicating matters, the initiative sponsors must submit signatures to each of the state's 58 counties, and county election officials have varying methods for validating signatures. The tribes recognized that they needed to collect a minimum of around 800,000 signatures to account for disqualifications, and all this had to be accomplished within a mere thirty days to prevent the federal closure of their casinos. This was an unprecedented challenge.

Leveraging the two million-name list developed from San Manuel's Norris and Seagal ads, the tribes swiftly gathered the required signatures within thirty days. This remarkable feat set a ballot qualification record that remains unrivaled to this day.

Acknowledging that this qualification could potentially lead to a change in the law, the federal government granted the tribe an extension beyond the date set for casino closures.

A Clash of Titans in the Golden State

The fate of Proposition 5, the Tribal-State Gaming Compacts Initiative, was a matter of immense interest, not only to California's tribes but also to some heavyweights in the casino industry. In October 1998, Las Vegas witnessed the grand opening of the Bellagio, an opulent $1.6 billion resort. Steve Wynn, a key player in this venture, had orchestrated a remarkable $12 billion revitalization of the Vegas Strip over the previous decade. With financial support from Michael Milken's bonds, Wynn unveiled the Mirage in 1989 for a staggering $630 million, followed by the $450 million Treasure Island Hotel and Casino in 1993. During the early '90s, Wynn also partnered with Gold Strike Resorts to establish a more budget-friendly casino where the old Dunes once stood.

Wynn wasn't alone in his interest in Proposition 5. Phil Ruffin, co-owner of the Trump International Hotel in Vegas with Donald Trump and owner of the renowned Circus Circus with its iconic permanent big top, also entered the arena. Both Wynn and Ruffin, billionaires, had previously collaborated through a partnership between Mirage Resorts and Circus Circus to construct the Monte Carlo Resort and Casino.

These moguls were dealing with substantial debts resulting from their extensive ventures. Their goal was to attract Californian customers, whom they believed were flocking to tribal casinos. To safeguard their market share, they were prepared to invest significant resources in the cause. They dispatched seasoned campaign professionals who ostensibly offered voluntary services, granted access to voter lists and other campaign assets, and pledged financial support against Prop 5. As per the California Fair Political Practices Commission, their recorded contributions amounted to $6,662,500 from Mirage Resorts, $6,512,500 from Circus Circus Enterprises, and approximately $6,500,000 from Hilton Hotels, which sought to retain Californian clientele for the Vegas Strip but played a less active role in the campaign. Smaller casinos like Sahara Gaming, Caesars ITT, Primadonna, and Stations chipped in with another $5 million.

Standing shoulder to shoulder with Nevada casino stakeholders was an unexpected coalition opposing Prop 5. This alliance included religious institutions, anti-gambling factions, labor union leaders, card clubs, and local casino development opponents. Additionally, five tribes, still favoring the Pala machine model and having secured their gambling arrangements with the governor, joined the opposition. Notably, Stand Up for California, a prominent anti-gambling community organization, chose to remain neutral, reluctant to align with the Nevada gambling proponents, and mostly stayed on the sidelines of the campaign.

While primarily funded by external gambling stakeholders, the opposition to Prop 5 warned voters of potential uncontrolled gaming expansion, drawing comparisons to the scale of Las Vegas and Atlantic City establishments. They stoked fears of organized crime-linked gambling infiltrating California. This unique coalition of Nevada casino magnates and anti-gambling advocates argued that the measure could introduce legal ambiguities, potentially allowing non-Indian entities to overshadow tribal casinos. They further contended that the initiative was both redundant and excessively expansive, opening the door for venues like bars, racetracks, and entertainment establishments to introduce gambling.

Critics asserted that the measure's regulatory exemptions could grant tribal casinos undue tax advantages and circumvent environmental regulations. Labor unions also claimed that it treated employees unfairly and eroded California's labor standards. Given that Wynn and Ruffin's Las Vegas establishments were unionized by HERE, both magnates and union leaders shared a vested interest in impeding the growth of tribal gaming in California.

The ballot argument against Proposition 5 stated:

> Proposition 5 isn't about allowing tribes to operate casinos on their lands. Federal law already guarantees that tribes can operate Indian casinos. Prop. 5 is a dramatic expansion of *unregulated, untaxed* casino gambling throughout California! Law Enforcement, Labor, Business, Seniors, Educators, Environmental and Local Government groups all oppose Proposition 5.

Supporting Proposition 5, Tribal advocates outspent their adversaries significantly. San Manuel was the top contributor with $27,783,000. Following them were the Morongo Band of Mission Indians with $12,621,000, the Viejas Indian Reservation at $11,012,000, the Pechanga Band with $9,709,92, the Agua Caliente Band at $2,317,000, and Barona near $1,000,000. Two other tribes, the Soboba Band and the Cabazon, each pitched in around $500,000. Miscellaneous contributions elevated the total support expenditure for the proposition to an unprecedented $63,238,000 in California's election history.

The Proposition 5 campaign championed the theme of Indian self-reliance. Advocates emphasized that the measure would enable historically marginalized Indian tribes to retain the economic progress they had achieved through gaming. They underscored how casinos had already halved unemployment rates on reservations and slashed welfare dependence by nearly 70%. Framed as a long-overdue opportunity for economic independence, Indian gaming was portrayed as a transformative force for California's tribes. Additionally, tribal leaders highlighted the creation of approximately 50,000 jobs benefiting both Indian and non-Indian Californians.

The ballot argument for the measure stated:

> Prop. 5 protects Native Americans' rights to have limited gaming, restricted to their tribal land. Prop. 5 promotes self-reliance among California's Indians, keeping them off welfare. Prop. 5 shares gaming revenue with non-gaming tribes for education and health programs and saves taxpayers hundreds of millions annually. Vote *yes* on 5.

A Dynamic Mix of Grassroots Mobilization and Media Outreach

The campaign to sway public opinion was a potent combination of grassroots mobilization and media engagement. Building upon the momentum generated by the 2 million Californians who had previously expressed their support for self-reliance through the Norris and Seagal commercials, we set the stage for a broader outreach.

A unified team of tribal leaders embarked on a comprehensive statewide tour, conveying a cohesive message to a diverse range of professional, civic, and fraternal organizations. The focus was on emphasizing the significance of backing Indian self-reliance. Engaging with the editorial boards of major and local publications further solidified support for Proposition 5 and its potential benefits to California.

The broad-based statewide backing highlighted an undeniable truth: when provided with information, the public recognized the mutual advantages of tribal self-reliance. Chairman Mark Macarro, alongside fellow tribal leaders, took center stage in television ads advocating for the proposition. These commercials not only reached a vast audience but also resonated deeply, a fact supported by ongoing surveys and feedback from focus groups.

Despite the expectation of a resounding victory, witnessing the measure secure a 62.4% approval rate, closely mirroring our preliminary survey estimates, was personally gratifying and a testament to the effectiveness of our survey research and collective campaign efforts.

The Do-Over – Challenging Proposition 5 in Court and Pursuing a Legislative Solution

As the initial excitement over the approval of Proposition 5 subsided, concerns arose regarding its constitutional validity. The Legislative Counsel had previously raised questions about potential conflicts with the California Constitution, particularly the prohibition of 'Nevada- and New Jersey-style casinos,' albeit without precise definitions. The crux of the matter revolved around whether the gaming styles authorized by the proposition might inadvertently create such casinos, putting it at odds with the State Constitution. Opponents had vowed to take this issue to the California Supreme Court if they lost at the polls. Tribal lawyers remained steadfast in their belief that their position was legally sound.

A coalition of residents and businesses, apprehensive about tribal plans to establish casinos near their communities, initiated legal action against Proposition 5. It was widely suspected that Nevada's gambling sector had financed this litigation behind the scenes. Prominent figures led the opposition, including Ted Olson, a prominent Washington D.C. attorney who would later serve as the U.S. Solicitor General. Simultaneously, the union HERE also filed a lawsuit, representing approximately 3,500 card club employees and 1,000 tribal casino workers. They argued that Proposition 5 violated California's labor protections.

On August 23, 1999, the California Supreme Court, primarily comprised of Republican appointees, overturned Proposition 5 with a 6-to-1 ruling. The court found that the proposition violated the state's constitutional prohibition on Nevada and New Jersey-style casinos. They argued that Proposition 5 had wrongly sanctioned previously prohibited slot machines and banked card games, explicitly forbidden by a 1984 constitutional amendment. Justice Kathryn Mickle Werdegar, in the majority opinion, contended that Proposition 5 "effectively endorsed outlawed casinos." In contrast, Justice Joyce Kennard, the lone dissenter, accused the court of disregarding the will of the people and their vote.

This ruling posed a significant setback for San Manuel and other tribes with gaming operations, as it opened the door for federal officials to close their casinos. The looming threat of federal attorneys shutting down tribal gaming establishments resurfaced.

Furthermore, there was a risk that the court's decision would impede ongoing negotiations with the Governor's office. These discussions, initiated by Proposition 5, aimed to establish tribal-state compacts and were already progressing at a deliberate pace.

Governor Davis acknowledged the court's decision but, recognizing the overwhelming public support for Prop 5, stated, "I am committed to exploring a constitutional approach aligns with clear desires of the people." Meanwhile, several legislative leaders voiced their support for the tribes, although skeptics contended that this support was influenced by substantial tribal contributions to their campaigns.

Ted Olson, representing residents and businesses opposing Proposition 5, argued that the court's ruling paved the way for legal challenges against any compact allowing casino slots and banked games, stating that "The governor cannot sanction casino-style gambling. What the tribes are engaged in, and aim to continue, is unequivocally illegal."

Mark Epstein, a legal representative for the tribes, emphasized that the battle was far from over and hinted at a new ballot measure, stating, "The tribes will once again present their case to the public, giving them a chance to modify the constitution." While some tribes contemplated an appeal to the U.S. Supreme Court, it was evident that this state law issue could only be addressed through a constitutional amendment. Consequently, San Manuel and other tribes explored avenues to amend the constitution's language.

California provides two methods to amend its constitution, aside from a constitutional convention: through a citizen-driven initiative or a legislative proposal. Following discussions with Governor Davis and supportive lawmakers, the tribes opted for a legislative amendment. With approval from both legislative chambers, this amendment would be presented to voters and, if passed, would modify the constitution. This approach bypassed the need for direct signature collection for amendments and carried the benefit of the State Legislature's endorsement. It required an extensive awareness campaign in Sacramento.

In collaboration with tribal leaders and their legal teams, lawmakers crafted Senate Amendment 11 to alter Section 19 of Article IV in the constitution, removing the ban on Las Vegas and New Jersey-style gambling. This amendment allowed the governor to negotiate compacts with federally recognized Indian tribes in California for the operation of slot machines, lotteries, and specific card games. These agreements would require legislative approval. With strong bipartisan support, the amendment cleared both legislative chambers and was positioned for a vote in March 2000 as California Proposition 1A: the Tribal Lands Gambling Amendment.

San Manuel and other supporters revisited the key messages that had previously rallied support for Proposition 5. Once more, the spotlight was on Indian self-reliance, especially in TV ads promoting the amendment. The official argument for the proposition read:

> Prop 1A prevents the shutdown of Indian gaming in California and promotes Indian self-reliance. It will allow Indian tribes to continue to have regulated gaming on their own tribal land to provide jobs and fund education, housing, and health care programs for gaming and non-gaming tribes.

Opponents of Proposition 1A voiced concerns about the potential for significant changes in California's gambling landscape, arguing that these changes could drastically reshape the state's character. Detractors made predictions that California could surpass New Jersey in slot machine numbers, with an anticipated addition of 265 new casinos to the existing 41. An influential anti-gambling group, Stand Up for California, played a pivotal role in mobilizing resistance, particularly in communities uneasy about the plans of local tribes to establish casinos. Other advocates against gambling cautioned that this could be California's last chance to avoid pitfalls like those experienced in Las Vegas.

Skeptics also raised questions about the motivations behind the initiative. Some questioned whether the Governor's support was driven by a desire to bolster his campaign funds. There were even insinuations that specific legislators had offered their support in exchange for contributions from gaming tribes, leading to suspicions of quid pro quo arrangements. These concerns added layers of complexity and controversy to the initiative's already heated debate.

The ballot argument against Proposition 1A claimed:

> Proposition 1A legalizes blackjack and up to 100,000 slot machines in California. Result: 214 authorized tribal casinos — some Las Vegas-sized, some run by Nevada gambling companies — paying no state or federal taxes on profits. We pay for costs of law enforcement and gambling addicts while casinos give millions to politicians.

Triumph of Proposition 1A: The Defining Moment for Indian Gaming in California

The campaign against Proposition 1A faced an uphill battle, struggling to gain momentum. Recognizing the likely outcome, Nevada's gambling stakeholders refrained from providing substantial funding, with records from the Fair Political Practices Commission (FPPC) indicating a meager contribution of just $3,783 against the proposition. In stark contrast, supporters of Proposition 1A poured in a substantial $23,923,458 to champion their cause. Among the tribes, the San Manuel Band of Mission Indians led the way with significant contributions of $8,711,261, followed by Morongo at $4,620,000, and Pechanga with $3,664,827.

The resounding voice of the people was unequivocal. On March 7, 2000, Proposition 1A secured an impressive 64.5% of the votes, surpassing even the level of support garnered by Proposition 5. At long last, Indian gaming in California received its legal endorsement, bringing an end to this chapter of the arduous struggle.

In the aftermath of these triumphant campaigns, there have been many individuals and groups seeking to claim credit for these victories. It is undeniably clear that the driving forces behind Propositions 5 and 1A were Ken Ramirez and the San Manuel Band of Mission Indians. Initially, they stood alone in their unwavering conviction, grounded in thorough research and a steadfast commitment to keeping their casino open defending tribal sovereignty. They faced formidable opposition from multiple quarters, including Las Vegas casinos, federal and state governments, labor unions, numerous cities and counties, and even some fellow tribes. It was only later that additional tribes, state legislators, and various stakeholders rallied behind the initiative, ultimately paving the way for tribal self-reliance through legalized gaming.

In the annals of history, the vision and fortitude of Ken Ramirez and the San Manuel Band of Mission Indians remain as the bedrock upon which Propositions 5 and 1A, and the path to tribal self-reliance, were firmly built. They stood as unwavering pioneers in the face of daunting opposition, championing tribal sovereignty and the cause of Indian gaming in California.

San Manuel in the New Century: From Triumph to Influence

San Manuel began to reap the rewards of its relentless pursuit to legalize tribal government gaming in California. The tribe's pivotal role in the two historic electoral campaigns earned them high respect among fellow tribal communities. Consequently, San Manuel's leaders consistently assumed leadership positions in tribal associations like TASIN and CNIGA. Beyond the tribal realm, their influence expanded as they received invitations to participate in various non-tribal organizations, underscoring both their success and the broader recognition of the positive impact of tribal gaming on California.

The tribe's political challenges persisted. With the recall of Governor Gray Davis, Arnold Schwarzenegger entered the gubernatorial race with a keen focus on California's economic well-being. He pledged to ensure that California Native American Tribes would "contribute their fair share" of revenue. Although the tribes had previously secured compacts with Governor Davis, they now faced the daunting task of renegotiating these agreements under Governor Schwarzenegger's more stringent terms. San Manuel recognized the precarious situation: if even one tribe agreed to the Governor's terms, it could potentially compel all tribes to follow suit.

To counter Governor Schwarzenegger's push for a larger share of tribal funds, San Manuel realized they needed to rally public support. Facing the iconic "Terminator" in the form of Schwarzenegger, who enjoyed widespread popularity, the tribe found itself not just opposing a governor but undertaking a formidable challenge. San Manuel's strategy was clear: demonstrate strength and unity to compel the Governor to reconsider his campaign.

To this end, San Manuel enlisted the support of a formidable and popular figure, Jesse Ventura — former Governor of Minnesota, Navy Seal, and Worldwide Wrestling Champion to stand up to "The

Terminator". In collaboration with Galanty & Company, a potent statewide television commercial was produced. Guided by survey insights and focus group data, Ventura highlighted Schwarzenegger's inconsistencies, firmly asserting that the tribes had indeed contributed their fair share. Within a mere week of its broadcast, Schwarzenegger abandoned his campaign, and the term "fair share from tribes" disappeared from his rhetoric. Ventura effectively conveyed to Californians the undue burden and injustices faced by California's Native peoples, reinforcing that they had been fulfilling their fair share all along.

Once perceived by state and federal officials as defiant, the tribe gradually built a reputation as a significant influencer in public affairs and inter-governmental relations. Initially starting in San Bernardino County, then expanding to the broader Inland Empire, and ultimately gaining statewide recognition, the tribe became a pivotal entity capable of addressing and contributing to major issues. An illustration of their elevated status was Governor Gavin Newsom's appointment of Chairman Ken Ramirez to his prestigious advisory board on California's future direction. Beyond the realm of politics, the tribe solidified its presence in the socio-economic fabric of the Inland Empire. The tribe consistently supported numerous charitable causes and non-profit organizations, annually donating millions of dollars to acknowledge other local entities making a positive impact in the community.

Pioneering Representation: James Ramos and San Manuel's Commitment to Native American Electoral Participation

San Manuel fully recognized the significance of political engagement and its power to influence policy. James Ramos, whose extensive record of service to the tribe included roles on the Business Committee and as Chairman, aimed to expand his contributions through a broader elected role.

Armed with an MBA from Redlands University, Ramos embarked on a campaign for a seat on the San Bernardino Community College

District Board of Trustees. His unwavering dedication and tenacity paid dividends, resulting in his election to three consecutive terms. Subsequently, he ascended to the position of San Bernardino County Board of Supervisors, eventually assuming the role of Chairman. In 2018, Ramos made history by becoming the first Native American elected to the California State Assembly, a milestone he repeated with his re-election in 2020. His legacy was further solidified when he became the inaugural Native American Chairman of the powerful Assembly Rules Committee.

Ramos played a pivotal role in urging Governor Newsom to acknowledge the profound injustices that California's Native Americans had endured — a historic first for any California Governor. Serving as a beacon of hope for Native Americans, Ramos consistently advocates for their active participation in public office and local governance. His remarkable achievements have inspired San Manuel to proactively support Native American electoral candidates across the United States, amplifying tribal voices and fostering increased tribal representation at every level of government.

Evolution of Tribal Governance at San Manuel

Three decades ago, my first visit to San Manuel revealed a tribal government operating from a modest two-bedroom HUD house. At that time, the entire workforce consisted of Tribal Administrator Geri Farr. Later, Lisa Buso joined the team, demonstrating remarkable dedication by continuing to serve the tribe to this day. San Manuel's remarkable journey to success is underpinned by a robust governance framework established by the tribe's constitution.

David Manzano, a member of the Business Committee, emphasized the importance of their role in shaping the future, stating, "With our rapid growth and significant changes, it was our duty to ask the tough questions that no one else dared to. We had to make sure we were getting the best information possible and the best value to make these difficult decisions."

The tribe's administrative structure revolves around two pivotal entities: the seven-member Business Committee, functioning as the tribe's executive branch, and the General Council, comprising all members aged 21 and above. The Business Committee members are elected by the General Council, and officer roles undergo a staggered four-year rotation. This elected committee shoulders a multitude of responsibilities, ranging from executing resolutions passed by the General Council and upholding by-laws to crafting policies, safeguarding business interests, affirming tribal sovereignty, and overseeing day-to-day tribal operations.

In a concerted effort to protect its sovereignty, San Manuel instituted a tribal judicial system, recently overseen by Chief Judge Claudette C. White. The Chief Judge and appellate judges are appointed by the General Council in collaboration with the Judiciary Committee. Additionally, pro tempore judges are appointed by the Business Committee, working in conjunction with the Judiciary Committee and the Chief Judge. This judicial system encompasses both a trial court and an appellate court, both under the guidance of the Chief Judge.

From Business Committee to Tribal Council

The entity once known as the Business Committee has now evolved into the esteemed Tribal Council, overseeing a myriad of specialized committees and programs. Within this council, tribal members often serve on multiple committees, and when electing council officers, experience is a key consideration.

Let's spotlight some of the notable leaders who have served within the Tribal Council:

- **Current Chairwoman Lynn Valbuena:** Chairwoman Valbuena boasts nearly five decades of dedicated service within the San Manuel tribal government. Her remarkable journey began as the Tribe's inaugural housing commissioner, and she has held various leadership positions within the Tribal Council, including

Secretary/Treasurer, Vice Chairwoman, and currently, she's in her fifth term as Chairwoman. Chairwoman Valbuena's influence extends beyond the tribe, with a 27-year chairmanship of the Tribal Alliance of Sovereign Indian Nations (TASIN). She has also held significant roles at both state and national levels, contributing to organizations such as the California Nations Indian Gaming Association, the National Indian Gaming Association, and the National Congress of American Indians. Her trusteeships include the National Museum of the American Indian, the Autry Museum, and an advisory council membership for the American Indian Chamber of Commerce of California.

- **Kenneth Ramirez:** Following Chairwoman Valbuena's leadership, Ken Ramirez took the reins as Chair. He is a committed public servant who has previously served five terms on the Committee as Tribal Secretary and held the role of Vice Chairman. Chair Ramirez's leadership extends across various fronts, including chairing the Education Committee, which oversees the San Manuel Education Department. He managed the tribe's television outreach and fostered partnerships with Loma Linda University to enhance healthcare and education accessibility. Ramirez also played a pivotal role in advocating for Propositions 5 and 1A on behalf of the tribe. Over three decades ago, he served as the inaugural General Manager of the tribe's bingo hall and casino.
- **Vincent Duro:** In 2020, Vincent Duro held the position of Vice Chairman, an office to which he had been elected for seven terms previously. His familiar face graced many educational and cultural TV commercials, as he played a crucial role in public awareness efforts related to first educating the public about tribal governments and the protection of tribal sovereignty.

- **Audrey Martinez:** With over three decades of tribal government experience, Audrey Martinez has served as Tribal Secretary and Tribal Treasurer. Her impressive resume and dedication to the tribe includes leading numerous significant tribal initiatives and outreach programs.
- **Latisha Casas:** Currently in her fifth consecutive term as the Tribe's Treasurer, Latisha Casas is unwavering in her commitment to ensuring the tribe's financial health and generational stability. Her leadership includes overseeing the Investment Board and chairing the San Manuel Gaming and Hospitality Authority, the entity behind the Palms Resort Casino.
- **Johnny Hernandez:** His remarkable journey within the San Manuel tribe started at the Bear Springs Hotel. He progressed to become Chairman of the Education Board and later served as Tribal Secretary on the Business Committee. Currently, Johnny holds the vital position of Vice Chairman, contributing significantly to the tribe's leadership and progress.

New Perspectives: The Business Committee has embraced fresh perspectives with the inclusion of younger members being elected to serve.

- **Alexis Manzano,** an alumnus of Claremont Graduate University and a Ph.D. candidate at the Drucker School of Management, brings academic insight and youthful vigor to the council.
- **Laurena Bolden,** serving her debut term as a Member-at-Large on the Tribal Council, has deep roots in San Manuel's educational and cultural spheres, contributing significantly to education and cultural direction initiatives.

These leaders, both seasoned and emerging, offer a harmonious blend of tradition and innovation within the Tribal Council, furthering the tribe's governance and community development objectives.

The Tribal Team: Navigating the Complexities of Governance and Gaming

In the intricate world of tribal gaming, expertise in casino operations is undoubtedly a paramount qualification for high-level staff appointments. The unique nature of tribal governments, their sovereignty, and the complex web of regulations surrounding tribal gaming necessitate a broader set of skills and knowledge. San Manuel, a trailblazing tribal nation in California, has recognized this need and has carefully cultivated a team of executives and professionals who not only excel in gaming operations but also possess a deep understanding of tribal governance and the tribe's cultural values.

At the heart of this successful leadership structure is the role of CEO. This position requires not only astute management of the casino's day-to-day operations but also a keen appreciation for the tribe's governmental functions and its commitment to sovereignty. Jerry Paresa, who served as CEO until 2018, is a prime example of this well-rounded approach. Paresa's journey with San Manuel began in 1989 when he started working at the tribe's bingo hall. Over the years, he took on increasingly pivotal roles within the tribe, including Executive Director of Government Operations and Intergovernmental Affairs. In 2000, he assumed the role of the casino's general manager, gaining invaluable experience in gaming operations. His appointment as CEO in 2009 was a testament to his expertise in both casino management and tribal government affairs. Tribal Chairman James Ramos, during the announcement of Paresa's appointment, emphasized the significance of his ability to navigate the intricate world of tribal politics, business, and community relations.

Loren Gill succeeded Paresa as CEO in 2019, having previously served as the casino's General Manager since 2015. Gill brought a wealth of experience in casino management, including roles in Las Vegas, which provided a valuable external perspective while respecting the tribe's unique culture and objectives.

Following Gill's tenure, Peter Arceo assumed the position of General Manager. His journey within San Manuel included serving as the Chief Operating Officer and, before that, as the Chief Marketing Officer. Arceo's experience spans various facets of the casino, and he brings a deep understanding of the tribe's values and goals to his role.

In 2020, Laurens Vosloo took the helm as CEO after serving as the tribe's Chief Financial Officer for six years. Vosloo's background includes executive positions at the Las Vegas Sands Corporation, a major player in the gaming industry. Notably, like several senior staff members at San Manuel, Vosloo is an alumnus of the University of Nevada Las Vegas, which is renowned for its gaming program. This academic foundation has undoubtedly enriched his understanding of the gaming industry, which he skillfully combines with his knowledge of tribal governance.

Within the broader context of tribal gaming operations, there has been a recurring challenge — the frequent turnover of executives. This phenomenon is often attributed to a mismatch between the expectations of corporate leaders and the realities of tribal governance. While many external executives bring extensive corporate experience, they may lack familiarity with the intricacies of tribal dynamics. They soon discover that managing a tribal enterprise demands a different set of skills than managing external corporate entities. Here, they are accountable not only to shareholders but also to a tribal government whose priorities may extend beyond the business bottom line. Tribal sovereignty, for instance, may outweigh profit considerations. This disconnect in understanding has led to strained relationships between some executives and their tribal employers. In these instances, these professionals may mistakenly perceive their academic and corporate backgrounds as superior, potentially undervaluing tribal perspectives. Understandably, this mismatch in alignment often results in executive turnovers, making way for leadership that resonates more closely with the tribe's overarching objectives and vision.

To address this ongoing challenge and ensure that future gaming industry leaders are well-versed in the intricacies of tribal governance, San Manuel took a proactive step. In partnership with Claremont Graduate University, the tribe established its Tribal Certificate Management program. This program is specifically designed for San Manuel's managers and executives, offering them a comprehensive education in tribal history, law, ordinances, and worldviews. Its primary goal is to instill in participants a deeper understanding of the nuances and responsibilities of operating within a tribal government framework.

This educational initiative underscores the tribe's foresight in equipping future gaming industry leaders with the right knowledge and perspective. The program's brochure aptly highlights its vision, emphasizing growth "through courses on tribal governments, Indian law, intergovernmental relations, Tribal sovereignty, management, and more!" Since its inception in 2006, the Tribal Certificate Program has not only grown but has also expanded its offerings to include an advanced course for its alumni.

San Manuel's approach to leadership in the gaming industry goes beyond traditional qualifications. While expertise in gaming operations remains a fundamental criterion, the tribe recognizes the essential value of a deep understanding of tribal governance and cultural values. Through a combination of careful executive selection and investment in educational initiatives like the Tribal Certificate program, San Manuel continues to lead the way in tribal gaming while maintaining its commitment to sovereignty and community values.

Governmental Affairs: Collaborative Leadership and Land Restoration

A pivotal chapter in the tribe's rich history of collaboration with local and regional entities is vividly exemplified by the narrative of the

Norton Air Force Base. This sprawling base, decommissioned in 1994, holds profound historical significance for the tribe, as it is recognized as an integral part of its Serrano heritage. In the early 2000s, tribal leaders embarked on a remarkable journey to actively shape the destiny of these lands. They initiated a collaborative partnership with the Inland Valley Development Agency (IVDA), marking the beginning of a shared endeavor to chart a course for development. Their unwavering efforts culminated in a historic milestone in 2005 when the Bureau of Indian Affairs (BIA) officially acknowledged the tribe's deep ancestral ties to the area. This acknowledgement led to the formal return of an 18-acre segment of the former base to the tribe, placing it in trust and thereby reestablishing a vital link to their ancestral past. This significant event underscores not only the tribe's unwavering commitment to preserving its cultural heritage but also underscores the power of collaboration in addressing complex land issues that have historical roots.

San Manuel's collaboration with IVDA transcended the confines of the 18-acre parcel. It extended to the ambitious transformation of the existing aviation facilities into the modern San Bernardino International Airport. This collaborative partnership serves as a prime example of how strategic alliances can be the driving force behind regional development and growth. During a media briefing where she discussed the tribe's substantial contributions and its vision for the land, Chairwoman Lynn Valbuena succinctly captured the essence of this partnership:

> "Since the closure of the base in 1994, San Manuel has been at the table with other governmental entities trying to map out what this region will look like in 10 and 20 years….As a recognized tribal government with a historical stake in the region, we have worked closely with the IVDA to not only plan for the future, but preserve and honor the legacy of air men and women, whose work was and continues to be an invaluable safeguard for our country."

San Manuel and the City of San Bernardino: Navigating Economic Challenges and Governance Complexity

The San Manuel tribal government maintains an exceptionally close and impactful relationship with both the City and County of San Bernardino. This association is particularly noteworthy considering the historical backdrop of economic struggles and political turmoil that have gripped this region.

San Bernardino, traditionally a blue-collar city, faced a significant economic decline as its industrial base eroded during the 1980s and 1990s. By the turn of the millennium, it had the unfortunate distinction of being among California's most economically challenged large cities. In 2013, grappling with insurmountable financial distress, the city took the unprecedented step of filing for Chapter 9 bankruptcy. This marked the onset of one of the nation's most protracted and complex bankruptcy cases, which would persist for four arduous years.

A substantial portion of the city's woes stemmed from its peculiar city charter, which lacked a clear and robust framework for mayoral leadership or a definitive mayor-council/city manager structure. Instead, it operated within a mixed system, where, for instance, the mayor appointed fire and police chiefs, subject to council approval. The police chiefs reported to both the mayor and the city manager, leading to potential conflicts and confusion regarding lines of authority. This administrative discord was evident in the tumultuous decade spanning from 2004 to 2014, characterized by a revolving door of leadership that witnessed five city managers, five police chiefs, four finance directors, and five public works directors. The city's inability to streamline its public staffing and effectively manage escalating public employee pension obligations were pivotal factors that pushed it toward the precipice of bankruptcy. Even after emerging from Chapter 9 bankruptcy in June 2017, economic challenges persisted. The onset of the Covid-19 pandemic further exacerbated the city's financial woes, raising the specter of potential insolvency once more.

A Strong Brand, A Resilient Tribe Committed to Community

In the face of their own challenges, including a three-month casino closure due to the Covid-19 pandemic, the San Manuel tribe demonstrated an unwavering commitment to their community. In September 2020, tribal leaders proudly unveiled Phase I of Mary's Village, a groundbreaking initiative funded by the tribe. Representing San Bernardino's first transitional housing dedicated to homeless men, Mary's Village goes beyond providing shelter. It offers comprehensive vocational training, job skills development, and holistic case management, empowering men with the tools for an independent future.

Recognizing the pandemic's disproportionate impact on the region's significant minority population, the tribe generously donated crucial protective equipment, including 3-ply surgical and KN95 masks, to local healthcare institutions. Throughout the year, San Manuel also made substantial contributions of food and essential items to the Riverside and San Bernardino branches of Feeding America. The Time for Change Foundation (TFCF) was another significant beneficiary of the tribe's support. TFCF is renowned for its efforts to reunite foster children with their mothers and for assisting nearly 2,000 women and children without shelter on their path to achieving stability and self-sufficiency.

The tribe and the city are forging deeper collaborations, exemplified by the extensive rehabilitation of Victoria Avenue, a major city thoroughfare, fully funded by the tribe for the benefit of all its users. This extensive project not only includes pavement repairs but also enhancements to sidewalks and sound barriers, covering the entire stretch from Highland Avenue to East Lynwood Drive.

Historically, many transactions between the tribal government and the city have centered around real estate. In 2017, San Manuel extended a $4.2 million grant to the San Bernardino Police Department, linked to a property exchange: the tribe relinquished its rights to a central 2.48-acre city plot, formerly housing a JC Penney department store. In return, the city transferred a 115-acre undeveloped area located in the San Bernardino Mountains' foothills to the tribe, towards the city's far northeast.

The tribe's influence extends not only within the City of Highland but also throughout the surrounding region. Eateries such as the Serrano Buffet, the Pines, RockN'Brews, Chingon's Kitchen, Tutu's Food Court, and Big Mo's are situated in Highland, reflecting the tribe's significant footprint. Their impact goes even deeper, with a substantial portion of the tribe's workforce of over 5,000 employees originating from the local community.

Beyond the immediate region in the Inland Empire, the tribe's name adorns several renowned establishments, both in the Inland Empire and beyond. They hold naming rights at the Staples Center in downtown Los Angeles and the Pond in Anaheim. Closer to home, the San Manuel Stadium in downtown San Bernardino stands as a testament to their influence, boasting an impressive 8,000-seat capacity. From 2008 to 2017, they held naming rights to a local 65,000-seat amphitheater. Their reach extends to Las Vegas, where they proudly sponsor the Allegiant Stadium, home to the Raiders professional football team.

Tribal Policies

The efficacy of a public affairs office is often the linchpin of an organization's external communication strategy. For San Manuel, this department stands out due to the leadership and expertise of its key players. Jacob Coin, as the Director of Public Affairs, brings a wealth of experience, skillfully navigating the intricate world of public relations and crafting strategic narratives that resonate with various audiences. His leadership has fostered a culture of excellence within the department, setting the bar high for impactful communication.

Complementing Jacob is Kenneth Shoji, the Public Information Officer. With a keen eye for detail and a deep understanding of the nuances of the industry, Kenneth ensures that the tribe's messages are not only heard but also resonate. His capacity to gauge public sentiment and tailor communications accordingly has proven invaluable in reinforcing the tribe's position in public consciousness.

Together, the synergy between Jacob and Kenneth has transformed San Manuel's public relations approach. Their combined expertise has elevated the organization's brand, forging stronger connections with communities and stakeholders alike.

During the height of the pandemic in mid-2020, San Manuel's profound and multifaceted involvement in public affairs was evident in the diverse array of stories emerging from their sophisticated media affairs office. Press releases, many accompanied by high-quality videos, shed light on different facets of the tribe's activities.

For starters, the tribe highlighted the remarkable achievements of its vast workforce of 5,000 members. From their participation in the LA Marathon, sponsored by the tribe, to the scholarships they secured for educational pursuits, awards garnered, and significant career milestones reached — each accomplishment was celebrated.

Additionally, the press releases highlighted a range of groundbreaking initiatives within the reservation. Noteworthy mentions included the San Manuel Fire Department's addition of a state-of-the-art tactical fire engine, the strategic use of extensive goat herds for wildfire prevention, and the casino's innovative protocols in response to the coronavirus pandemic.

Moreover, the media affairs office dedicated efforts to spotlight and commemorate pivotal events like Juneteenth, National Forest Day, and Veterans' Day, emphasizing their cultural and historical importance.

The tribe ardently pursues its policy objectives in the realms of education and health, investing substantial resources to bring them to fruition. In the educational arena, the tribe has two primary focal points. Firstly, they prioritize the nurturing of future gaming industry leaders. Secondly, they champion the empowerment of Native Americans to celebrate their heritage and educate both their own community and the broader public about their history and culture.

San Manuel Casino, along with the tribe's other economic ventures, is not merely a business entity. It represents tribally owned enterprises that necessitate a workforce attuned to the nuances of Native American concerns. This philosophy is evident in their generous support for professional training programs at the University of Nevada, Las Vegas. In 2019, the tribe generously endowed $9 million to UNLV, laying the foundation for a chair in tribal gaming and bolstering online courses centered on tribal gaming operations. Numerous San Manuel staff, many of whom are UNLV alumni, surely appreciated the tribe's dedication to bolstering the university. Chairwoman Lynn Valbuena, while announcing the donation, expressed:

> "In the tribe's history, tribal government gaming is the only tool that has worked to meet our economic development objectives. Yet, the full potential of tribal gaming cannot be achieved if we do not also place emphasis on developing Native people to manage our economic developments, including gaming. Therefore, we are making this investment in the partnership with UNLV to educate and prepare our children, grandchildren, and future generations to help chart our path to a sustainable future."

In 2019, the tribe generously donated $5 million to Arizona State University, backing the Indian Gaming and Tribal Self-Governance initiatives housed within the Sandra Day O'Connor College of Law.

San Manuel's educational philanthropy also seeks to encourage Native Americans to embrace their rich heritage while simultaneously enlightening the broader community about the poignant history of California tribes. They've endorsed a number of academic programs dedicated to Native American Studies across different universities, including one at UC Riverside. They have also provided scholarships to tribal students enrolled in this program. Furthermore, the University of Redlands received a significant grant in support of a comparable initiative. As expressed in the press release:

> "We are committed to the development of leadership outreach to prospective Native Students throughout Southern California. In doing so, we have awarded the University of Redlands a $5.9 million grant to advance and support Native scholarships, programming, and outreach. With this grant, we strive to inspire and connect an estimated 280,000 prospective Native students and their families from Los Angeles, Riverside and San Bernardino counties to a best-in-class private university where students can flourish in a safe, supportive environment as they pursue a higher education."

In recognition of the establishment of California Native American Day in 1998, San Manuel has championed a week-long educational endeavor annually at California State University, San Bernardino. This initiative aims not only to celebrate this pivotal acknowledgment but also to equip educators with the resources and knowledge needed to accurately teach about local Native American history in their classrooms. The annual events are led by facilitating hands-on learning experiences, creative workshops, edutainment, and featuring Native music. The events have educated thousands of fourth-grade students, their teachers, and the wider community about California's indigenous roots.

Since 2008, the San Manuel tribe has been a steadfast supporter of the Barcid Foundation's Native Youth Multimedia Workshop. This initiative is tailored to impart skills in acting, writing, directing, camera handling, and video editing to Native American youths residing in both reservations and urban hubs. The overarching goal is to inspire these youths to envision and embrace careers in television, film, and emerging multimedia platforms. Additionally, from 2009 onwards, San Manuel has backed the Ambassador Program by Americans for Indian

Opportunity. This program not only promotes cultural understanding but also extends vital assistance to the areas in direst need, including the Navajo Nation and the urban Indian enclave of Albuquerque.

In its persistent endeavors to spotlight Native American concerns, the San Manuel tribe actively championed Assembly Bill 1460. This bill mandates that all students across the 23 campuses of the California State University complete a three-unit ethnic studies course, offering choices between Native American, African American, Asian American, or Latina and Latino studies. Concurrently, at the national level, the tribe endorsed crucial legislation, notably "Savanna's Act" and "The Not Invisible Act". Expressing gratitude, they acknowledged President Trump for ratifying these acts that aim to support the communities, families, and victims of Murdered Missing Indigenous Women and Girls. Furthermore, in 2018, tribal leaders stood in solidarity with the Department of Veterans Affairs (VA) Secretary Robert Wilkie to inaugurate the construction of the inaugural American Indian Veterans Memorial at Riverside National Cemetery.

Health and wellness hold paramount importance for the tribe. They've embraced a trailblazing healthcare concierge program, pioneered by my company, that ensures their members have access to premier doctors and top-tier care, eliminating any obstacles in the healthcare for tribal families. In a recent philanthropic endeavor, San Manuel generously donated $14 million to Claremont Graduate University. This contribution was aimed at streamlining their diverse academic programs in public health, especially targeting underserved communities. Additionally, the tribe extends financial support to several health clinics in the Inland Empire, notably including the Riverside-San Bernardino County Indian Health and the Native Challenge Program.

The tribe has a rich history of backing medical initiatives through their philanthropic endeavors. In 2016, they forged a partnership with Loma Linda Hospital to establish its inaugural health center in downtown San Bernardino. Beyond the establishment of the health center, their generosity laid the foundation for the San Manuel Gateway College. This institution was envisioned to enhance health screening education and provide pivotal organization-wide training. The primary mission of the San Manuel Gateway College is to equip the Inland Empire with foundational job training and education in the realm of healthcare. Commemorating a century-long collaboration with Loma Linda University Health in 2019, the tribe furthered its commitment by donating a staggering $25 million in support of the Loma Linda University Children's Hospital. Additionally, the tribe actively supports the Susan G. Komen Inland Empire, including its pivotal "Fundamental Treatment Assistance Program."

The casino, with its array of restaurants and stores, is just one facet of San Manuel's expansive business endeavors. Over the years, especially after their statewide measures passed, the tribe has delved into real estate investments. In Highland, they've spearheaded a 12-acre mixed-use development project known as San Manuel Village, which boasts a hotel, conference center, a diverse range of eateries, retail outlets, and office spaces. Furthering their foray into hospitality, the tribe introduced the Bear Springs Hotel — a luxurious boutique retreat nestled in the San Bernardino Mountains' foothills. Positioned strategically off Highway 330, this hotel is envisioned to be the preferred gateway for those heading to the mountain resorts.

Beyond their core ventures, the tribe has expanded its portfolio with a 25-acre administrative and storage facility at Sterling and 5th Street, offering comprehensive warehousing solutions. In Washington DC, they've capitalized on the rising property values with ownership of the Residence Inn Capitol and a sizable 12,000 square-foot office building. Furthermore, they hold the title for another Residence Inn in Sacramento.

San Manuel's footprint isn't limited to real estate. Their presence in the sports arena is notable, with investments in esteemed teams like the Las Vegas Raiders and San Diego Chargers. They also have stakes in prominent venues like the Orange County Anaheim Pond, the base for the Anaheim Ducks, and the iconic Staples Center, which hosts games for both the Los Angeles Lakers and Clippers.

San Manuel's tribal leaders are hard-headed entrepreneurs who invest for the long term — for generations yet unborn.

San Manuel's World Views

Through numerous interactions with tribal leaders, I've gleaned insights into the core principles and beliefs that shape San Manuel's discussions and decisions. It's essential for managers within the organization to grasp these foundational tenets to effectively navigate their roles, boost business revenue, and align with the tribe's overall objectives. Here are select excerpts from speeches, press releases, and interviews that encapsulate these guiding thoughts.

> ***Sovereignty.*** "We began as free and independent people on lands that were ours alone. Today, we are sovereign on tribal land. Sovereignty is the basis of all our work for this generation and all to come."
>
> ***The Earth.*** "As the Yuhaaviatam Clan of the Serrano people, we share a worldview that the stewardship of the earth is a duty that is Creator-given. The tribe honors its ancestral lands in the San Bernardino National Forest. We are spiritually rooted in these lands — they define and sustain us."
>
> ***Past and Future Generations.*** "Our elders suffered so much to help us. We must work to do the same for all future generations?"
>
> ***Health.*** "Ensuring the health and safety of the tribal community, as well as the greater community is our duty. Providing assistance and sharing resources to benefit the health and wellness of our neighboring communities is an ancestral value ingrained in the San Manuel culture."

> ***Tribal unity.*** "We are strong only when we are together. Strength and unity are driven toward a future of success, built upon collaboration and commitment for all."
>
> ***Equality.*** "Native Americans believe we have a moral and spiritual kinship and responsibility for all people of the world. As a people united with all Americans and world citizens, we renew our commitment to social justice and equality. We believe in fairness to all."

Drawing from their rich history and deep-rooted values, San Manuel has weathered numerous challenges. These foundational principles have not only sustained them through past struggles but remain the guiding compass steering their present and future policies and decisions. As they move forward, it's these unwavering beliefs that will continue to anchor them, ensuring they remain resilient, purpose-driven, and impactful creating a recognized legacy.

CHAPTER FOUR

Jamul Indian Village of California

The major participants in this case history may be briefly described.

The Tribe

The Jamul Indian Village of California traces its lineage to the indigenous Kumeyaay people, also known as the Tipai-Ipai. For over 12,000 years, Kumeyaay ancestors have thrived in the region encompassing the northern boundary of present-day Baja California in Mexico, extending into what we now know as San Diego County. The Kumeyaay, who communicated in a dialect from the Yuman-Cochimí language group, were identified by the Spanish as either the Kamia or the Diegueño. The latter designation was derived from the Mission San Diego de Alcala, established in 1769 — a year that many Kumeyaay view as the onset of their adversities.

The Kumeyaay, renowned among ethnologists for their intricate gourd artistry and the evocative melodies of their Bird Singers, have long used ceremonial songs to impart life lessons and ancestral wisdom across generations. Historically, Kumeyaay villages congregated to host multi-day fiestas, celebrating with shared meals, dances, and rites. These gatherings persisted into modern times, serving not only as cultural touchstones but also as means of economic sustenance and trade forums. Early European explorers, whom the Kumeyaay termed 'Gucamal', initially engaged in trade with them. Over time, these explorers' pursuits forced the Kumeyaay eastwards into areas like El Cajon, Santee, Jamacha, and Jamul, as well as into less favorable regions in Baja.

In the 1980s, a transformative moment arrived for the Jamul Indian Village when it finally gained access to electricity and running water on their reservation in East County San Diego. These basic amenities, often taken for granted in most of San Diego, had a profound impact on the tribe's way of life.

The introduction of electricity and running water allowed the Jamul Indian Village families to come together in even more meaningful ways. It not only enhanced their day-to-day living conditions but also strengthened their sense of community and connection. With the power to illuminate their homes and access clean, running water, the tribe experienced an improved quality of life that facilitated gatherings, celebrations, and communal activities.

This newfound access to modern utilities symbolized progress and development for the Jamul Indian Village, marking a significant step toward improving the living standards and overall well-being of their community. The availability of electricity and running water laid the foundation for a stronger, more interconnected tribal community, fostering a sense of unity and empowerment that would play a pivotal role in their journey towards self-reliance and economic prosperity.

The Kumeyaay inhabit five communities in Baja and maintain presence across thirteen reservations in San Diego County. In San Diego, besides the Jamul, the Kumeyaay communities are affiliated with several federally recognized tribes: Barona Group, Campo Band, Capitan Grande Band, Ewiiaapaayp Band, Inaja Band, Iipay Nation, La Posta Band, Manzanita Band, Mesa Grande Band, San Pasqual Band, Sycuan Band, and the Viejas (Baron Long) Group.

Among these thirteen bands, six — including the Jamul Indian Village which oversees the Jamul Casino — currently operate successful casinos in San Diego County. These establishments are Barona Casino and Hotel-Resort in Lakeside; Golden Acorn Casino by the Campo Band, straddling the San Diego and Imperial County border; Valley View Casino by the San Pasqual; Sycuan Casino in El Cajon; and the Viejas Casino in Alpine. The challenging landscape of the casino industry is highlighted by the 2012 shutdown of the La Posta Casino. The potential for growth in the sector is underscored by San Pasqual's dual ventures: its Valley View Casino and its involvement in a development corporation managing various casinos and hotels.

"As we champion the rights of the Jamul Indian Village, we're also standing up for all Americans. We take immense pride in our service to our country," emphasized Tribal Chairwoman Erica M. Pinto.

Within the heart of the Jamul Indian Village resides a community with a deep and enduring commitment to serving our nation. It's a place where pride in military service runs through the very fabric of the tribe. In fact, it's been noted that the Jamul Indian Village boasts more veterans per capita than any other tribe in California.

These veterans are not just statistics; they are a source of immense pride and celebration. Each year, the Jamul Indian Village comes together to honor their veterans, those who have served with distinction and honor. Among them is former Chairman Kenneth Meza, a true hero who earned the distinguished Purple Heart for his unwavering bravery.

In the Jamul Indian Village, service to the country is not just a duty; it's a tradition, a legacy, and a testament to the enduring spirit of this remarkable community.

In San Diego County, the Kumeyaay aren't the only tribal entities who have ventured into the casino industry. The Rincon band, part of the federally recognized Luiseño Mission Indians, oversees the operation of Harrah's Resort Southern California, formerly known as Harrah's Rincon Resort and Casino. Located in Pauma Valley, the Pauma Band — another segment of the Luiseño Mission Indians — manages Casino Pauma and its associated ventures. The Pala Indians, with a lineage tracing back to both the Cupeño and Luiseño tribes, run a casino and resort on their expansive reservation nestled in the San Luis Rey River Valley. These diverse gaming establishments, all within a convenient hour's drive, are dotted throughout San Diego County, offering a vast array of entertainment options.

Furthermore, San Diego County also hosts several non-tribal gaming establishments, such as the Lucky Lady Casino, Palomar Card Club, and Seven Mile Casino. These non-tribal venues often find themselves at odds with tribal gaming operations, resulting in ongoing disputes and legal battles.

Consequently, San Diego County presents a plethora of gaming venues, both tribal and non-tribal. While convenience, location, and accessibility are pivotal for the success of these establishments, the high level of competition within the county underscores the importance of other offerings. Factors like diverse culinary experiences, entertainment, the variety of gaming options and other choices play a crucial role in drawing patrons to their preferred gambling destinations.

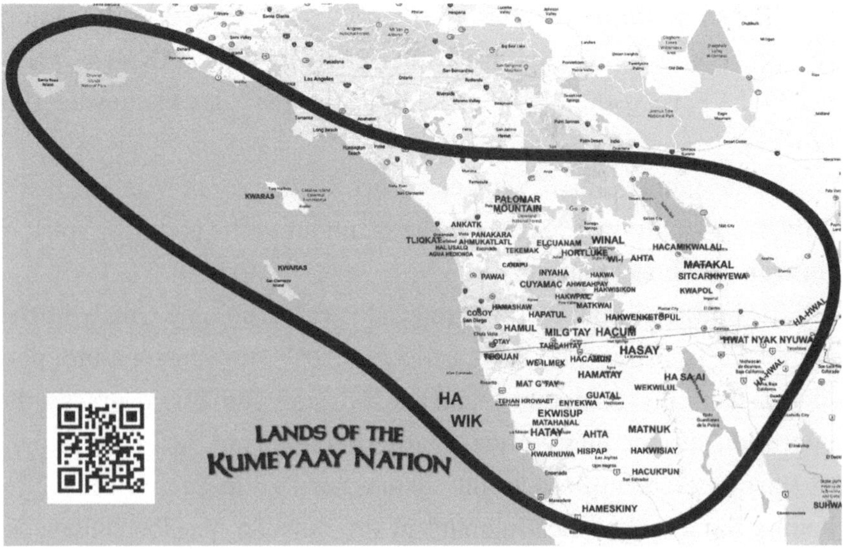

The success of a casino often pivots on its geographical placement. Accessibility, surrounding attractions, and transportation routes play a paramount role in attracting both locals and tourists. For instance, the Lucky Lady Casino enjoys a prime position, being only a 20-minute drive from central San Diego when one takes the I-85 and College Avenue. This proximity to the heart of the city means it's not only convenient for local residents but also for tourists staying in downtown accommodations.

Conversely, the Rincon Band's Harrah's Resort, situated 50 miles from San Diego, has had to strategize differently. While it might be farther from San Diego's core, its accessibility to other significant population hubs becomes a game-changer. Tourists form a significant segment of casino-goers, and this resort caters to them effectively. Notably, visitors from both San Diego County and neighboring Orange County can reach the resort with relative ease, thanks to the connectivity provided by California State Route 76.

Moreover, the resort's partnership with the renowned Harrah's brand has provided it with a competitive edge. This association lends a trusted reputation and brand recognition, ensuring that customers are more inclined to make the longer journey. The brand's pull can be felt especially among tourists and those from Orange County who might recognize and trust the Harrah's name, thus considering the drive worthwhile.

In the intricate dance of location and branding, a casino's success is often shaped. While proximity to urban centers can be a boon, strategic partnerships and excellent transportation links can level the playing field, even for those situated farther afield.

During this period members of the Jamul Tribal Council included: Kenneth Meza, Bill Mesa, Carlene Chamberlain, Raymond Hunter, Adolf Thing, Eleanor Miller, Erica Pinto, Robert Mesa and Michael Hunter.

Gaming in San Diego County

The Jamul Indian Village, situated less than 20 miles from the heart of San Diego City, holds the distinction of being the nearest tribal casino to this bustling metropolis. On a day with minimal traffic, the drive to this destination is a brisk 33 minutes via the I-5 or a slightly quicker 31 minutes if one chooses the California 52 East route. Highway 94 leads you directly to the casino. Without this direct access from its reservation, the feasibility of Jamul's casino would be in jeopardy.

Although Jamul isn't an incorporated city, it's recognized as a Census Designated Place (CDP). As of the 2010 census, its modest population stood at 6,163 residents. But it's the casino's proximity to San Diego's metropolitan area, home to over three million people, that gives it a significant competitive advantage. This edge is hinged on one critical factor: the ease with which patrons can journey to the casino and gain entry to the reservation.

County Official Exerting Power

In California, the practical execution of most governmental functions doesn't emanate from the state capitol, Sacramento. Instead, these responsibilities fall under the jurisdiction of one of the state's 58 county governments. Areas such as public health, law enforcement, elections, tax collection, and social services are predominantly managed at the county level. This county-centric approach is even more pronounced in unincorporated regions where no city governance or direct oversight exists.

Each county government typically operates under a five-member board of supervisors. These supervisors are elected based on distinct supervisorial districts. A common sentiment is that a county supervisor in California can amass significant power and exercise it with fewer checks and balances than most other elected officials.

San Diego County's District 2, encompassing Jamul, is the county's most expansive supervisorial territory, stretching over 2,000 square miles. Representing this vast district, with its 620,000 residents distributed among numerous cities and vast unincorporated areas, often provides an elected supervisor with a significant degree of electoral security.

Throughout the duration of this case history, Diane Jacob served as the supervisor representing District 2 on the San Diego County Board of Supervisors. A pivotal point to note regarding Supervisor Jacob is her personal connection to Jamul. She resides there on her family's ranch, making the Jamul Indian Village not just a part of her designated district, but also, quite literally, her neighbor. The reservation's proximity to her residence underscores its significance in her purview.

Diane Jacob began her career as a local schoolteacher and progressively became involved in school district politics. By 1987, she was elected President of the California School Boards' Association. Her ascent continued in 1992 when she secured her position as a County Supervisor. Despite facing two redistricting challenges, Jacob maintained her seat, serving an impressive seven terms and becoming the longest-standing member on the San Diego County Board of Supervisors. This longevity amplified her influence within the Board. Her reign concluded in 2020. Although Measure B, ratified by 68.27% of voters in June 2010, imposed term limits, it permitted Jacob and two other sitting members an additional ten-year tenure.

An unwritten rule among the Board is a mutual deference, where supervisors typically uphold decisions of colleagues affecting only their respective districts. In matters concerning the Jamul casino, Jacob's voice resonated as a representative for the entire Board, and key stakeholders recognized her authority. Notably, while she publicly endorsed Indian gaming within the county and supported other casino ventures, she remained unwavering in her opposition to a casino in Jamul.

CalTrans: Navigating California's Transportation Landscape

Since the 1960s under Governor Pat Brown's leadership, California's state government has been segmented into overarching 'super-agencies' or cabinet-level collectives, often identified by acronyms like CalEPA or CalGovOps. One such super-agency is CalTrans, the California State Transportation Agency.

Overseeing the state's mobility, safety, and air quality, CalTrans is composed of eight sub-agencies. These include the California Highway Patrol (CHP), the Department of Motor Vehicles (DMV), and notably, the California Department of Transportation, which also goes by the moniker CalTrans.

This department takes charge of the state's public airports, inter-city rail, and over 50,000 miles of highways and freeways. Emphasizing its commitment to safety and efficiency, its website portrays it as a "performance-driven, transparent, and accountable" body, dedicated to enhancing the state's economic stature and quality of life.

With a workforce of 21,000, CalTrans operates on an annual budget of $15 billion.

Typically, the person at the helm of CalTrans possesses a civil engineering degree or has specialized expertise in transportation. Although primarily a bureaucratic role, it has its share of political challenges. Issues like road maintenance deficits and deteriorating infrastructure have added to the complexities of transportation politics. Stationed in Sacramento and heavily reliant on legislative funds, CalTrans is susceptible to political influences. Its sizable budget attracts intense lobbying, and the director's dismissal can serve as a convenient political move for higher-ups. During the course of this narrative, the leadership at CalTrans witnessed frequent changes. Under Governor Jerry Brown alone, the position saw five different occupants: Will Kempton, Randall Iwasaki, Cindy McKim, Malcolm Dougherty, and Laurie Berman.

CalTrans functions through 11 designated districts, usually led by individuals with expertise in transportation. These districts maintain regular communication with local authorities, with county supervisors often emerging as pivotal players. Located on Taylor Street in downtown San Diego, CalTrans District Number 11 is conveniently close to the office of Supervisor Diane Jacob. During the period leading up to 2018, the district was managed by Laurie Berman, who later briefly held the position of CalTrans director. It's reasonable to assume that Berman frequently liaised with Supervisor Jacobs and her team, including on matters related to the Jamul Casino.

The Bureau of Indian Affairs (BIA)

The BIA's influence in matters related to land-into-trust decisions and state-tribal compacts significantly elevates its stature among Native American leaders. Even though its administrative rank means that it operates under the supervision of the Assistant Secretary for Indian Affairs and its actions are reviewed by the National Indian Gaming Commission, its impact is undeniable.

It's evident that many Native Americans with political aspirations aim for positions such as the Assistant Secretary, Indian Commissioners, and BIA Director. The trend over recent years highlights this: the last 13 individuals appointed as Assistant Secretaries were of Native American descent; a majority of recent NIGC commissioners have tribal affiliations; and most directors of BIA share the same heritage. A review of the biographical data for these roles over the past 25 years reveals a diverse representation from tribes such as Menominee, Pawnee, Chickasaw, Lac Courte Oreilles Chippewa-Choctaw, Oneida of Wisconsin, Sault Ste. Marie Chippewa, Oglala Lakota Sioux, Fort Peck Assiniboine, and Taos Village.

While California tribes aren't explicitly mentioned, they consistently work to cultivate relationships within the administrative ranks. Many tribes retain lobbyists boasting unique connections to senior BIA officials or pivotal staff members. Legal experts versed in trust matters are often engaged to advocate before the BIA, frequently with a strategic emphasis on advancing legal challenges. Established casino-operating tribes, wary of potential competitors, strategize to sway administrative decisions against emerging gaming tribes. In essence, the interplay of politics and tribal gaming competition heavily impacts BIA decisions.

Investors in Tribal Gaming

The Jamul Indian Village showed remarkable determination in their journey to find the right investor for their casino project, persisting for over two decades with unwavering standards and a commitment to open the best Indian casino in San Diego county.

Investors in tribal gaming face high risks, with roughly 20% making profits. Many contracts get terminated or bought out by tribes before the seven-year limit set by the National Indian Gaming Commission.

Investors in tribal gaming are acutely aware of the unpredictable nature of contracts in this arena. An illustrative case is when Donald Trump was a business partner with the Twenty-Nine Palms Band of Mission Indians in the Trump 29 Casino, situated in the Coachella Valley.

When Trump encountered financial troubles and declared bankruptcy, the tribe saw an opportunity to assert its sovereignty and protect its investment. In a bold move, they decided to terminate their three-year association with Trump. One of the most symbolic actions they took was promptly removing his name from their casino. This incident underscores the dynamic nature of tribal partnerships and the tribes' assertive stance in safeguarding their interests and sovereignty.

Given such scenarios, investors aim for contracts that not only cover their expenses but also offer substantial management fees, ensuring a return on their investment. This cautious approach reflects the understanding that tribal gaming ventures can be intricate and subject to unexpected shifts in partnerships, making contractual terms a crucial aspect of their investment strategy.

The NIGC sets limits on fees tribes can offer management companies, preventing exploitation and ensuring tribal communities benefit most, aligning with its commitment to safeguard Native American rights and finances.

Sometimes, tribes establish lasting partnerships with investors, as exemplified by Harrah's and the Rincon Band of Luiseno Indians in Valley Center. Most tribes adopt their name for the casino, not only for branding but also to emphasize the tribe's presence as a local entity, employer, and longstanding tribal authority in the area.

In the early '90s, Jamul's first investor was Palace Station from 1993 to 1994. Palace Station, a Las Vegas hotel and casino under Station Casinos, saw potential in San Diego's Indian gaming boom. Despite their inexperience in tribal gaming, they proposed a partnership with Jamul. This short-lived alliance dissolved in 1994 due to challenges faced by Jamul.

Following this, the tribe partnered with Indian Gaming of America (IGA) from 1994 to 1997. IGA acquired land for the tribe, and despite a brief financial dispute later, the tribe settled the matter.

In 1997, Kevin Kean partnered with Lyle Berman and Lakes Gaming for Jamul. Berman, an avid poker player, began his career in his family's business, Wilson's Leather. Later, he co-founded Grand Casinos, aiming to revolutionize gaming beyond Atlantic City and Las Vegas. They ventured into Mississippi's riverboat casinos and pioneered tribal gaming.

Hilton Hotels acquired Grand Casinos in 1998. Grand retained tribal gaming, becoming Lakes Gaming under Berman's leadership. Lakes emerged as a top tribal gaming investor, even managing Red Hawk Casino for the Shingle Springs Band of Miwok Indians.

In 2015, Lakes acquired Golden Gaming and re-branded as Golden Entertainment. Berman served as chairman and CEO. By 2017, Golden Entertainment diversified into Nevada casinos, reducing its tribal gaming focus with Berman stepping down as CEO.

Kevin Kean has a background in commodity futures trading where he leveraged his extensive investment network to assist Indian tribes in their casino endeavors. His expertise and trustworthiness established him as a reliable advisor to tribal communities, aiding them in land acquisition, federal recognition, and negotiating tax and gaming agreements. Kean's portfolio includes partnerships with major gaming establishments linked to the Coushatta and Tunica-Biloxi tribes. Teaming up with Lakes Gaming, he played a pivotal role in projects with the Shingle Springs and Jamul Indian Village in California. With three generations of tribal support in his family history, Kevin maintains a deep connection to tribal communities across the country.

Penn National Race Courses (PNRC), in operation from 2013 to 2019, was the fourth investor group involved with Jamul. Originally focused on horse racing in Pennsylvania, PNRC expanded its reach under CEO Peter D. Carlino during the 1970s. It entered the casino industry, acquiring properties in St. Louis, Biloxi, and Baton Rouge. In 2003, the company acquired Hollywood Casinos, marking a significant shift away from its equestrian roots. Recognizing the potential in online gaming, PNRC saw Jamul as a gateway to California's growing online gaming market.

In 2005, PNRC acquired Argosy Gaming for $1.4 billion, plus an assumed $791 million in debt, making it one of America's top gaming companies, trailing only Harrah's and MGM Mirage. By 2016, the company had also added Las Vegas' Tropicana to its portfolio.

Unlike Lakes, PNRC had no prior experience with tribal casinos and was primarily focused on online gaming.

After over two decades of struggle and determination, on October 10, 2016, in partnership with the Jamul Indian Village of California, Penn Gaming introduced Hollywood Casino Jamul, marking a momentous occasion for the tribe. The Indian Gaming Regulatory Act (IGRA) stipulates that investors can have no more than seven years for their management agreements with tribes. Typically, tribes strive to buy out their investors as soon as possible. For Jamul, this occurred less than two years after the casino's opening. By mutual agreement, Penn Gaming and the tribe terminated their arrangement on May 23, 2018.

It was a moment of pride and trepidation for the Jamul Indian Village, as this marked the first time, they had complete ownership and control of the casino. Their initial action was to re-brand and rename it as the Jamul Casino.

The Case History

The Jamul Indian Village had a modest beginning. The tribe, grappling with poverty, did not receive formal recognition for their reservation until 1981. Tribal leaders, including Vice-Chairman Kenneth Meza, Executive Council Member Carlene Chamberlain, Jesse Pinto, and Raymond Hunter, have vivid memories of how their reservation came into being. A particularly enduring memory is of Raymond Hunter's uncle, Hank Aldama, tasked as a child with marking the reservation's boundaries. Told to pick up a small rock and run in all directions until he could no longer, his efforts determined the span of their lands. Looking back, Mr. Aldama said with a laugh, "I thought I ran farther than that."

The tribe made every effort to thrive on its modest six-acre reservation in east San Diego County. While most of San Diego County including their neighbors in Jamul enjoyed modern conveniences, the tribe waited longer for electricity, running water and indoor plumbing. Carlene Chamberlain recalls times when water was sourced directly from wells, carried home in five-gallon buckets. Homes were rudimentary, assembled from available scrap plywood and metal, some with dirt floors. A nearby creek served for washing and bathing. It was only in 1980, as recalled by Mr. Pinto and Mr. Meza, that they first experienced the benefits of electricity. Traditional practices like bird singing, basket weaving for barter, hunting, fishing, and tribal games defined their way of life, with frequent gatherings for peon tournaments being a highlight. Today, these valuable traditions are being safeguarded and promoted, as exemplified by Tribal gaming.

Tribal Councilmember James Cuero III and tribal member Christopher Pinto proudly represent the Jamul Indian Village at Kumeyaay events, teaching the youth, ensuring that the customs of old are passed down to the next generation.

"The annual "All Souls Day" on November 2nd is a heartfelt tribute to those who walked before us,' said Erica Pinto. This day sees tribal members cleaning the cemetery, placing vibrant flowers on the graves, and as night falls, lighting candles by the headstones. "It's lighting a path for our ancestors to come home," said Vice Chairman Kenneth Mesa."

For Carlene Chamberlain, this annual ritual holds deep significance. She frequently reflects upon the trials and tribulations faced by her ancestors. "Without their sacrifices and their resilience, we wouldn't be standing here today," she often muses. Her memories paint a vivid picture of a time when aspirations like secure housing, education, and comprehensive health-care were distant, almost unattainable. For her, these traditions are not just rituals but a bridge to the past, ensuring that the newer generations never forget the struggles that paved their way. As Carlene said, "every lit candle and every placed flower are a silent thank-you to those who came before."

Recognition, Land and a Tribal Constitution

The late 1970s and 1980s were crucial for the Jamul Indian Village's quest for recognition. In 1978, the BIA listed the criteria a tribe needed to achieve federal recognition status. The Jamul elders, had been preparing for this moment having worked for this for generations, presented their evidence in 1979. By 1981, their efforts paid off: the tribe was formally acknowledged by the federal government, cementing the Jamul Indian Village of California's sovereign status. "Our ancestors passed down the knowledge that in our struggle for sovereignty, our traditions and our unity were our greatest resources," said Kenneth Meza.

Without a reservation, tribal sovereignty is meaningless. Land is essential for the exercise of self-determination. Many federal programs and benefits hinge on having a reservation or trust land combined with federal recognition. While it's undisputed that the tribe's ancestors have lived in what's now San Diego County for over 12,000 years, and specifically in Jamul for many decades, it's also a legal fact that federal recognition paves the way for the restoration of tribal homelands.

It's impossible to discuss the progress of the Jamul Indian Village of California without talking about tribal administrator, Julia Lotta. Often seen as the tribe's guiding light, Julia's relentless commitment to upholding tribal sovereignty is what made the difference. Her combined expertise in research and diplomacy positioned her as an indispensable asset to the tribe. Her sole pursuit has always been the tribe's welfare and advancement. For those who cross her path, Julia's presence is powerfully felt — she truly is a force of nature.

In 1981, concurrent with its federal recognition, the Jamul Indian Village was granted six acres of trust land in eastern San Diego County. This was the smallest land grant among the 18 San Diego tribes. While the land had no utilities, agricultural potential, or resources, and only hosted a few trailers, it was still home to the Jamul Indian Village.

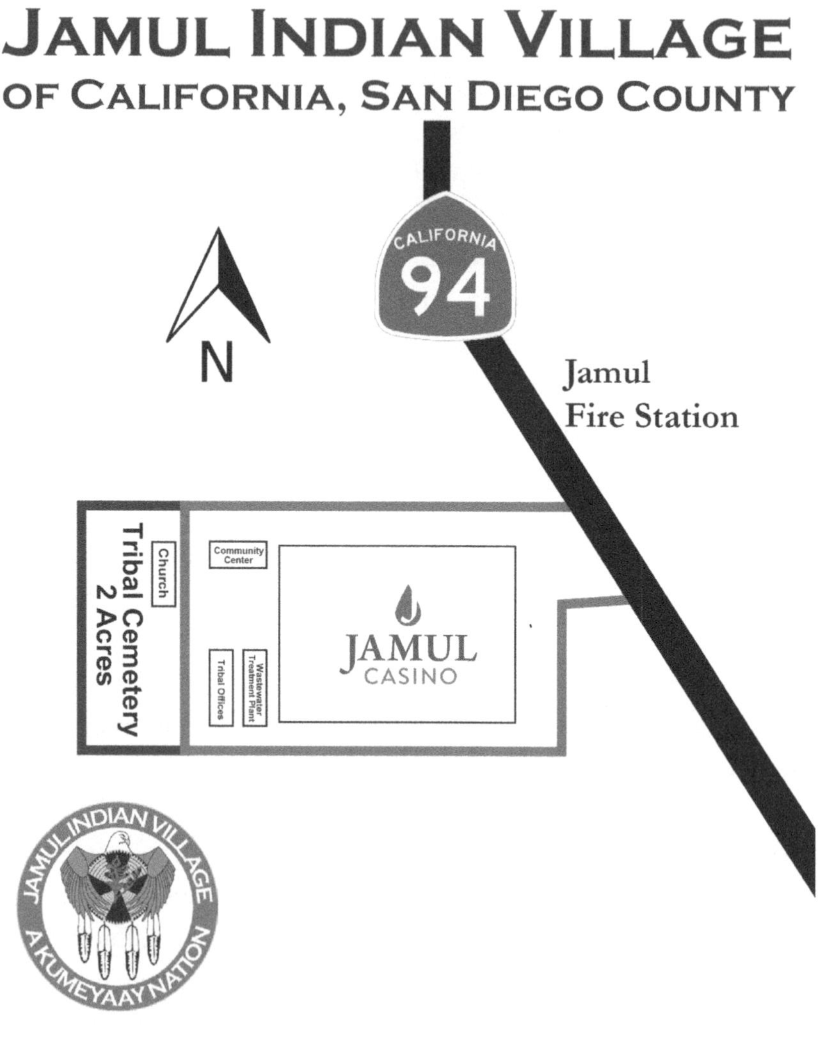

As they pursued recognition, the tribe formulated and adopted the Jamul Indian Village of California Tribal Constitution, outlining the laws and governance procedures for its tribal government. The Constitution states that the tribe's governance lies in the hands of the General Council, consisting of all eligible voters aged 18 and older, currently numbering 71 members. This General Council is steered by the Tribal Council, an elected group of seven members, which serves as the face of the tribal government, executing decisions made by the General Council and other assigned tasks.

Dreams of Gaming

While several California tribes ventured into bingo, Jamul's sparse local clientele meant they couldn't follow suit. When the Sycuan Band, another Kumeyaay tribe, opened their 'bingo palace' in 1983, the Jamul elders saw little chance of replicating such success. Their community's economic outlook appeared grim.

As the 1980s progressed, the Jamul elders observed notable shifts in tribal gaming. While the Cabazon decision and the introduction of IGRA initially didn't ignite much hope, by 1988, the landscape began to change. The Sycuan's expansion into slot machines and, notably, the Viejas tribe's casino announcement reignited the Jamul elders' aspirations. Amidst this, they also recognized a growing tension around the state's gaming future.

Elected in November 1991, Governor Pete Wilson was opposed to casino gaming that was bringing in vast profits for tribes in Connecticut. Despite his stance, some California tribes had already embraced casino gaming, pressing forward even as they faced legal opposition and shutdown attempts by local sheriffs. In San Diego County, the Sycuan and the Viejas tribes ran profitable operations, with the latter even inaugurating a modern slot-focused facility during Wilson's campaign.

Seeing these developments, the Jamul elders started to entertain the idea of their own casino. The idea became an urgent plan. Recognizing the need for local non-Indian support, they initiated efforts to raise awareness about their tribe, its rich history, and its significance in both Jamul and San Diego County.

A Tribal-State Compact and Propositions 5 and 1A

Noticing its strategic location near the urban hub of San Diego, Jamul engaged legal experts and began preliminary discussions with an outside investor, Indian Gaming of America. The roadmap, as guided by the IGRA, was ostensibly simple: to establish a casino, a tribe needed to finalize an agreement with the state and collaborate with local governments. If other tribes could navigate this, how hard could it be for Jamul?

Their initial goal was to expand their six-acre trust land for casino and parking infrastructure. This meant dialogues with potential investors to determine how much land was needed and financing options for the land and to build a casino. In this pivotal phase, Chairman Kenneth Meza, Vice-Chairman Bill Mesa, Carlene Chamberlain and the tribal council collaborated with tribal attorney Gene Madrigal, a distinguished member of the Cahuilla tribe, renowned for his representation of various tribes and his extensive expertise in Federal Indian law. This was a significant and challenging moment for the Jamul tribe. They embarked on a strategic mission to negotiate with the State, marking a critical point in their journey.

As Jamul was taking its initial steps, the legal landscape for Indian gaming in California was shifting dramatically. In November 1998, Proposition 5 won the approval of California voters, amending the state law to allow tribal casinos to host slot machines and banked card games which was immediately overturned. By 2000, Proposition 1A amended the state's constitution, granting casino privileges exclusively to tribes. Governor Wilson's resistance was overruled by California tribes' success. Governor Wilson lost the battle, the California tribes won!

United in their objectives, tribal leaders, both from existing gaming tribes and those hoping to open casinos, chose to negotiate California's inaugural compacts collectively. This strategy aimed to consolidate their collective power in discussions. Jamul was among the 57 tribes actively involved in the dialogue with California's executive branch.

The tides shifted in November 1998 with the passage of Proposition 5, a win that strengthened the tribes' negotiating stance. On that very day, Gray Davis was elected to step into Pete Wilson's shoes as Governor. Sacramento's buzzing corridors often echoed with a curious statistic: more Californians had cast their vote for Proposition 5 than for Gray Davis himself, underscoring the tribes' political clout. Gone were the anti-gaming eras of Deukmejian and Wilson, replaced now by a gaming-friendly executive.

Unified in purpose, a coalition of tribes, each aspiring for their compact with the state and wary of a potential federal clampdown on gaming, found common ground. Together, they decided to engage in collective negotiations with state representatives.

Yet, the discussions unfolded on various planes, revealing nuances and cracks within the tribal coalition. Given the sheer number of stakeholders involved, space limitations at the negotiation table became a genuine concern. Imagine a gathering of elders, legal representatives, and consultants from myriad tribes, totaling over a thousand individuals, each bound by their obligation to consult with their tribal communities. The dynamics of these negotiations were anything but straightforward.

Two distinct groups, with shifting membership, played pivotal roles during these negotiations. The first group, with a changing roster, actively participated in the actual negotiation sessions. Meanwhile, the second group, also marked by evolving membership, was tasked with conveying potential decisions to the multitude of tribal members unable to attend these sessions. This often led to calls for the negotiators to alter their course or for a reconfiguration of the negotiation team.

Leaders from the Jamul Indian Village of California were part of this intricate negotiation process, which unfolded relentlessly, operating nonstop, seven days a week, week after week throughout 1999. The negotiations generated a vast volume of information, which was meticulously processed and disseminated to each tribal government. This monumental undertaking involved thousands of individuals, each tribe diligently pursuing the most advantageous tribal compact possible.

On September 10, 1999, leaders from 57 tribes, including the Jamul Indian Village, gathered with Governor Gray Davis in Sacramento to sign historic documents that endorsed tribal gaming and set forth its conditions. This compact remained in effect until 2020. Despite this agreement, California's laws still prohibited slot machines and casino-style games. Therefore, the tribes needed to overcome one final obstacle: a statewide ballot measure to amend the constitution and permit such gaming.

In response to tribal lobbying, the State Legislature introduced SCA 11, which outlined the ballot language for Proposition 1A. This proposition asked the people of California to vote on changing the state constitution to allow tribal gaming. In the 2000 primary election, this last hurdle was successfully cleared when Proposition 1A passed on March 7, with over two-thirds of California voters in favor. Remarkably, voters in San Diego County were even more supportive of gaming than other areas of the state, as both Propositions 5 and 1A received over 70% of the local vote.

With the law and public sentiment in San Diego firmly behind Indian gaming, one question lingered: Could anything now stop the Jamul Indian Village from realizing its casino dream?

The First Casino Plan and Its Opponents

In 1999, the Jamul Indian Village made a significant announcement regarding their intention to develop a new hotel and casino. This marked a shift from their previous investor, IAG, to Lakes Entertainment, a well-respected company with a strong presence in tribal gaming. Lakes committed to covering an initial investment of $200 million and offering professional management for the gaming operations.

Jamul was not alone in its pursuit of gaming prosperity within the San Diego region. Besides the already successful casinos operated by the Sycuan and Viejas tribes, several others, including Rincon, San Pasqual, Pala, Barona, and Pauma tribes, possessed the necessary land

and had plans to open their casinos in 2001. This raised a pressing question: How many casinos could the San Diego market sustain?

This question weighed heavily on investors as they had to account for construction, development, operational, and ongoing expenses. The specter of competition potentially eroding their profits loomed large. Tribal elders, particularly those from the Sycuan and Viejas tribes, along with their investors, began to worry that their customer base might shift to these new facilities. Surveys conducted by business consultants appeared to confirm that casino location and travel convenience significantly influenced the number of gaming customers. Investors started calculating driving distances from densely populated areas in the county to these newly planned casinos. The most substantial potential competition seemed to emanate from Jamul, as its casino would be easily accessible from major urban areas in San Diego County.

Reports consistently reached Jamul's elders regarding opposition, often covert, within the local community, including other gaming tribes in San Diego. It was widely talked about that paid lobbying endeavors were underway in Sacramento and even in Washington DC with the aim of halting or delaying Jamul's casino project. Lakes Entertainment, with its extensive gaming network, grew increasingly concerned about the potential for costly delays at various stages of securing BIA approval.

One of the opposition strategies became public knowledge when Viejas formed an alliance with Supervisor Jacob. Their tactic involved an attempt to compel Jamul to merge its reservation with the Ewiiaapaayp Band of Kumeyaay Indians. Attorney Madrigal reassured Jamul's elders that this effort was unlawful and bound to fail. Nonetheless, it was a ploy that needlessly postponed the development of the Jamul casino, leading to costly and unnecessary litigation.

"We knew we had to make changes as we were facing difficulties. It was a moment to defy expectations and stage a remarkable comeback," said Vice Chairman Bill Mesa.

The tribe had carefully crafted its casino plan with guidance from Lyle Berman, Tim Cope and Lakes' seasoned gaming executives. They emphasized that the key to the casino's profitability lay in maximizing the number of slot machines on the gaming floor. Consequently, a larger casino was deemed more advantageous. To accommodate a substantial number of visitors, ample parking space would be essential. Moreover, in line with various business studies suggesting that high-end hotel facilities could offset the challenges of commuting for gaming patrons, the plan included a 15-story hotel and 500,000 square feet of gaming space. All these factors necessitated an expansion of the initial six-acre reservation. The plan required the BIA to take into trust an 81-acre tract adjacent to the existing reservation.

The necessity for acquiring new reservation land exposed the project not only to local opposition but also to negative lobbying efforts at the BIA. The immediate and highly visible reaction came in the form of protests led by residents of Jamul and the surrounding area.

In defense of their plan, Jamul turned to surveys that had been employed in the campaigns for Propositions 5 and 1A. These surveys had consistently indicated broad public support for gaming as a means of tribal self-reliance. They also demonstrated that voters believed casinos could generate new jobs in communities, contribute additional funding to State and local governments, and aid in supporting local charities. An analysis of election data revealed that Indian gaming enjoyed the backing of over 70% of voters in San Diego County, marking one of the highest support rates among all California counties. Jamul emphasized these points in its press releases. In the tribe's public relations efforts to secure support from the local community, particularly one facing economic challenges, significant emphasis was placed on the assertion that the casino would create more than 2,000 well-paying new jobs. Additionally, the tribe committed to enhancing local public safety and fire protection for the entire community.

Not surprising, "NIMBY" (Not In My Backyard) was a major factor in Jamul. Those who could have potentially taken these casino jobs did not voice their opinions during the immediate community reactions following the announcement. Instead, the protests were led by individuals who had moved to Jamul for its rural lifestyle, were content with their current circumstances, felt threatened by a development they believed might diminish their property values, and held negative attitudes toward gambling and gamblers. It's worth noting that statistics show many of these protesters had voted in favor of Propositions 5 and 1A. In fact, Supervisor Diane Jacob, one of the most visible opponents, was on the record as a strong advocate for Indian gaming in the State and had expressed support for other San Diego County casinos.

The local opposition to Jamul's proposed casino exhibited elements of 'Nimbyism,' epitomized by figures like Supervisor Jacob, who owned and resided on a nearby ranch. It was also grounded in well-structured and reasoned arguments. The primary concern voiced consistently and vociferously was the anticipated impact on traffic along Highway 94, the town's main road and the sole route for potential customers to access the planned hotel and casino. Adding to this concern, Highway 94 narrowed to just two lanes near the casino site, leading to amateur estimates circulating about potential traffic congestion at various times of the day. Consequently, the initial calls for official traffic studies by CalTrans were made by opponents of the Jamul project.

Another prominent theme in the protests revolved around the strain expected on fire and police services. The East County region faced annual threats from brush fires, and the arrival of gamblers, some of whom might be unaware of or indifferent to fire risks, was portrayed as a potentially dire problem. Critics contended that issues like prostitution and drug-related activities, which they attributed to casinos, would overwhelm local police and sheriff services.

Environmental concerns also played a significant role in the opposition. 'Light pollution,' referring to the nocturnal obscuring of the starry sky due to the hotel and casino lighting, was one of the cited environmental threats. Additionally, worries centered on the increased water usage impacting the local aquifer, heightened air pollution, and the potential disruption of local wildlife habitats. Recognizing these concerns, the Jamul Indian Village announced its intention to prepare and produce an environmental impact report aimed at addressing all these issues comprehensively.

"Those of us who are fortunate to live in Jamul love it. Over the last two decades, Jamul has transformed from a sleepy town into a thriving community, with new parks, wineries, restaurants, and commercial developments. It continues to grow, offering wonderful opportunities for all its residents. Jamul is now the premiere place to live," said Tribal Chairwoman Erica M. Pinto.

Outreach Efforts Versus Litigation

As local opposition in Jamul to the casino project intensified, Jamul Indian Village adopted an extensive program of community engagement. The core belief was that effective communication with the broader Jamul community, as well as with various political and bureaucratic entities, could help mitigate opposition, and ideally, garner support for the tribe's development plans.

The tribe made concerted efforts to connect with influential figures in the wider San Diego-area business and civic circles, aiming to secure their endorsement for an economic development initiative centered around the proposed casino. Many of these figures had previously supported other tribes in San Diego County in their endeavors to establish Indian casinos. Furthermore, the outreach program sought to educate all segments of the public about the tribe's deep historical roots in the local area.

Various initiatives were undertaken, such as public meetings, participation in Rural Fire Protection District (RFPD) board and local planning group meetings, responding to numerous letters and inquiries, collaborating with a team of highly experienced consultants, and conducting comprehensive environmental studies. The tribe also made a commitment to ensure that the public had ample opportunities to provide feedback on the project.

Despite these efforts, the local opposition to the casino remained largely unaltered. In its most detrimental manifestation, opposition resulted in litigation filed by San Diego attorney Patrick Webb. Ultimately, Webb, who had strong local connections, including with Supervisor Jacob, filed more than 40 lawsuits. Initially, these suits were directed at the Bureau of Indian Affairs (BIA), asserting that Jamul Indian Village was not a legitimate tribe and did not possess a genuine reservation. These claims were consistently dismissed by judges due to their lack of legal merit and factual inaccuracies. They likely drew the attention of BIA officials to the local controversy surrounding Jamul.

A pivotal event occurred on February 7th, 2003, when the BIA conducted a meeting in Jamul to discuss the environmental impact report produced by the tribe. Numerous Jamul residents attended to voice their opposition to the casino, while supporters highlighted the potential community benefits, including job creation and increased entertainment options. In summary, local opponents predominantly argued that the casino would irrevocably alter the character of their rural community and that a 15-story hotel was grossly out of place in Jamul. Although known supporters in the audience struggled to sway opponents, it's evident that their perspectives reached the BIA, which continued to collaborate with the tribe throughout this process.

This particular BIA meeting solidified opposition and catalyzed the formation of a local organization called 'Jamulians Against the Casino,' which later adopted the name the 'Jamul Action Committee' (known by the acronym JAC). Shortly after this meeting, the BIA announced its denial of the additional 81 acres, delivering a significant setback to both the tribe and its investor.

Falling Behind the Competition

In 2001 and 2002, four new casinos emerged in San Diego County: Pala Casino in early April 2001, followed by Campo Band's Golden Acorn Casino, Rincon's Harrah's Resort, San Pasqual Band's Valley

View Casino, and Pauma Band's Casino Pauma. Despite prior amicable relations, the competitive nature of the gaming industry positioned these neighboring tribes, along with Sycuan and Viejas, as potential rivals.

Faced with the finality of the BIA's denial of the 81-acre addition to the reservation, Jamul had to rethink its strategy. Collaborating with Lakes Entertainment, they revised their plan to fit the existing six acres. This updated proposal featured a 12-story hotel and a six-story casino, reflecting input from the community. Despite expecting continued local opposition, a symbolic groundbreaking event occurred at the reservation on December 10, 2005.

Attorney Webb initiated more lawsuits, financially supported by Jamulians Against the Casino and other local anti-gaming groups, and publicly endorsed by Supervisor Jacob. While all of Webb's suits were eventually dismissed, they incurred expenses, delays, and increased costs for Jamul's investors.

Webb's most critical lawsuits involved the BIA and CalTrans, both posing significant threats to Jamul. The BIA's decisions could be influenced by Jamul's gaming competitors, and CalTrans was sensitive to San Diego County government and Supervisor Jacob. Whether due to Webb's lawsuits or Supervisor Jacob's pressure, CalTrans took a firm stance against Jamul's use of Highway 94. They argued that 'public safety' necessitated the construction of a driveway to the casino from Melody Lane, a side road, at a cost of millions for the tribe. When the tribe proposed installing stoplights in the middle of Highway 94, CalTrans insisted on expensive environmental impact studies before permitting such an installation.

Jamul's chairman and council, observing that CalTrans hadn't imposed obstacles on other new casinos in the county, alleged that the agency was succumbing to pressure from Supervisor Jacob. They also claimed that attorney Patrick Webb received support from Jacob in his lawsuits aimed at compelling CalTrans to prioritize public safety by denying casino traffic access to Highway 94.

At this point, the tribe started discussing potential legal actions with its attorney, Gene Madrigal. They began assessing the likelihood of taking CalTrans to court for infringing on their constitutional sovereignty rights.

To appease local sentiment, Jamul initially decided to hold another public meeting with residents to address community concerns. In collaboration with Lakes Entertainment, they developed artistic renderings of the proposed casino buildings, and a court reporter was hired to record comments.

The meeting held on September 13, 2006, revealed continued community support for the group Jamulians Against the Casino, who opposed the tribe and the proposed casino. Of the 40 speakers at the meeting, less than a third expressed support for the plan. The main points of contention remained Highway 94 and the expected increase in traffic.

Under the leadership of Jamul's new chairman, Leon Acebedo, who would later become the Executive Director of the California Nations Indian Gaming Association, the tribe now fully comprehended that their opponents' strategy aimed to delay development until their investor's patience and resources were depleted. Further delays would mean falling even further behind the competition. The possibility began to emerge that Jamul's compact with the State might expire before any gaming facility could be constructed.

"We knew we had them right where we wanted them," said Chairman Leon Acebedo.

Fighting Back or Surrendering?

By this point, there was no denying that Supervisor Jacob was at the forefront of local opposition to the casino. She openly expressed her views and actively lobbied against the casino project in San Diego, Sacramento, and even Washington D.C. She had famously stated that the casino would be built "over my dead body." Her support for Patrick Webb's lawsuits, which continued to drag the tribe (and its investor) into costly legal battles, was no secret. The tribe believed her influence had played a role in the difficulties they faced with CalTrans in Sacramento and the BIA in Washington D.C. There were even attempts to incite dissatisfaction among tribal members and encourage opposition to the casino project.

In a show of determination, the tribe decided to take the initial steps toward casino construction. On March 10, 2007, they evicted three residents who were not recognized tribal members and who had expressed opposition to the casino: Karen Toggery, her son, and Walter Rosales, who had been residing on the Jamul reservation. Local Jamul residents, including leaders of JAC, gathered to protest these evictions and entered the reservation to do so. The Sheriff, a vocal opponent of the casino project, expressed concern over the public unrest.

To maintain order, the tribe hired a local security firm. When protesters persisted in entering Tribal land and ignored requests to leave, these security guards resorted to using pepper spray and metal batons to ensure the safety of tribal members and property. The escalating tensions were a clear sign that controlling the situation was becoming increasingly challenging.

Both sides believed they were in the right: Gene Madrigal could advise the tribe on their sovereignty over their land, while County lawyers could equally advise Supervisor Jacob on the authority to maintain peace. In a contentious meeting, Chairman Acebedo and the Supervisor agreed to a cooling-off period. The Chairman signed an agreement, witnessed by the Supervisor, stating that the homes of the evicted individuals would not be demolished for at least seven days.

It didn't take long for Chairman Acebedo, growing increasingly frustrated with the questioning of the tribe's sovereignty on their own land, to regret his compliance. Two days later, he ordered the demolition of the homes, fully aware that it would spark further controversy in the community.

At this juncture, it appeared that some in the tribe were willing to concede that building a Class III casino might be an insurmountable challenge and that pragmatism demanded a partial retreat. This perspective seemed to prevail when, immediately after the homes were demolished, Jamul released a statement indicating that they no longer wished to negotiate with California. Instead, they claimed they were planning a casino with only Class II games, which would be exempt from state control or regulation. Yet, for others in the tribe, this was viewed as a strategic withdrawal, with plans to continue the campaign until victory was achieved.

Navigating the Roadblocks: The Battle with CalTrans

It wasn't just some tribal members who were unwilling to give up on the dream of a Class III casino; the investor also had compelling reasons to persist. By this stage, Lakes had invested around $50 million in the Jamul project. If nothing more than a Class II facility (involving Bingo games, not traditional slot machines) were to be constructed, they would never recoup their substantial investment. Gene Madrigal, too, was highly motivated to continue the fight, as he believed that Indian law and the U.S. Constitution strongly favored Jamul.

With professional support from Lakes and Madrigal, the tribe reengaged in negotiations with CalTrans. The agency maintained its unyielding position, leading the tribe to file a lawsuit against CalTrans on October 1, 2008. Essentially, Jamul's argument was grounded in their sovereignty, asserting that they had the right to utilize their land as they saw fit within the bounds of the law. Therefore, CalTrans' demand to construct a driveway from Melody Lane was viewed by the tribe as "improper meddling by the state." The tribe saw this lawsuit as a 'must-win,' as did their investor. Carlene Chamberlain, a member of the tribe's Executive Council, emphasized the critical importance of this lawsuit at the time, stating: "Lakes Entertainment can't secure funding for design and construction until it's certain that gamblers will have access to the slot machines."

CalTrans, however, steadfast in its commitment to public safety, refused to grant permits for stoplights on Highway 94 without further environmental impact studies. Behind the scenes, Supervisor Jacob and other leaders of the opposition understood that traffic was the Achilles' heel of the casino project. They believed that additional Environmental Impact Reports (EIRs) could be utilized to demand new road infrastructure and inflate costs to the point where the tribe's investor would be compelled to abandon the project.

In reality, the tribe opted for another strategic retreat and reached an agreement with CalTrans to conduct an EIR. This was a potentially expensive concession with potentially adverse consequences. On April 7, 2009, the tribe entered into a Settlement Agreement with CalTrans. Subsequently, on March 12, 2009, Lakes Entertainment released a review of their 2008 results, indicating that the Jamul project would be 're-evaluated' considering the altered financial landscape and would be 'closely monitored.' They reduced the "fair market value" of the Jamul project by 80% and postponed the projected completion date to 2014. Opponents perceived these actions as the project's last struggles, merely preliminary steps toward its ultimate abandonment.

Death and Resurrection

On March 13, 2012, Lakes Entertainment terminated its development contract with Jamul Indian Village. The investor had poured $57 million into the project, a substantial portion of which went toward legal fees. There was no resolution to the traffic predicament, and local opposition remained unrelenting.

At this juncture, it speaks volumes about the tenacity of the Jamul leadership that they refused to concede defeat. In the wake of Lakes' withdrawal, the tribe announced their intention to collaborate with the local community to design a smaller Class III facility. They made commitments to address the concerns voiced by Jamul residents.

"Our ancestors fought for us, and my mother reminded us that our only path to succeed was to keep fighting as we have the law on our side, said Erica M. Pinto.

Formidable challenges lay ahead. A new compact needed to be negotiated with the State, yet Jamul's opponents had already demonstrated their substantial influence in the corridors of power in Sacramento. Finding a new investor was another hurdle, as the gaming industry had become aware of the project's difficulties, and the tribe still owed Lakes $57 million. On the traffic front, CalTrans had essentially emerged victorious, and it seemed that only significant investments in new road infrastructure would secure State approval. Furthermore, Supervisor Jacob and a coalition of local opponents continued to obstruct the project.

After extensive preliminary negotiations, the tribe entered into an agreement with Penn National Gaming, a company with no prior experience in tribal gaming, to become their new investor. Penn also committed to assuming the $57 million debt while serving as the developer and manager of what they unveiled as a $400 million 'Hollywood Casino' in Jamul.

Projected to open in mid-2016, the casino was slated to feature a three-story gaming and entertainment complex spanning approximately 200,000 square feet. This facility would encompass gaming areas, restaurants, bars, and requisite parking. Penn estimated that the project would generate around 2,500 jobs, both in construction and permanent positions, within the region. Construction of the casino commenced on January 11, 2014.

In less than a month, on February 6, the Jamul Action Committee took the matter to federal court by filing a lawsuit against the National Indian Gaming Commission and the BIA. Their claim rested on the assertion that the tribe was not "under federal jurisdiction" in 1934, which, they argued, meant that the reservation's trust status was invalid. If upheld by the court, this claim would have spelled the end of any prospects for a casino. While their legal defense eventually prevailed, it did impose both financial costs and time delays on the tribe.

To address CalTrans' concerns and appease the local community, the tribe entered into agreements to allocate $20 million for infrastructure improvements to local roads. These funds were earmarked for enhancing intersections, adding lanes and turnouts, and generally enhancing road safety through upgrades. A dozen intersections were identified for improvement, and the completion of the first four received strong community support and approval.

The subsequent batch of intersections involved land owned by prominent casino opponents. These individuals refused to cooperate with the tribe on land rights and attempted to impede intersection upgrades. Advised by their legal counsel that they could force the tribe into violating the compact, thereby derailing the casino project, they refused to engage in discussions with the tribe. Lawsuits were filed, injunctions were sought, and the tribe was effectively held hostage, with demands for millions of dollars in exchange for the 20-30 feet of real estate required for the improvements. Even today, long after the Jamul Casino has opened, these lawsuits remain unresolved in California courts.

The County Sheriff remained staunchly opposed to the casino. He emphasized concerns about DUIs, drug abuse, and petty crime, warning that he would block the road — the main entrance to the reservation — to prevent public access if called upon.

Nothing the tribe or Penn could do or promise seemed to appease this small but persistent group of local opponents. In January 2015, Glenn Revell, President of the Jamul Action Committee, stated to the Union Tribune, "This is not about an Indian project." He contended that his group "would oppose a commercial development of this size, in this location by anyone," adding, "We do not believe it fits the character of the community and are concerned that the traffic cannot be mitigated to the extent it does not exacerbate the challenges faced by emergency responders." Revell pointed out that his 'action committee' had filed multiple lawsuits, including one against Caltrans over traffic concerns and another in federal court seeking to disqualify the property from gaming.

On March 11, 2015, the East County News Service reported that approximately 200 protesters staged a "flash mob" demonstration in Jamul, wearing red as they continued to voice their opposition to casino construction. The protesters carried signs with messages like 'No Casino, Not Now, Not Ever' and 'Not anti-Indian, anti-Casino.'

The editor of Deerhorn Valley Antler reported that two motocross bikers attempted to disrupt the protesters by riding close to them, "spraying rocks, dirt, and gravel" on those standing closest to the site. The local paper also noted that a petition drive had been initiated to gather signatures from casino opponents, "although it is unclear what impact signatures could have on a project under construction and reportedly on track to open next year, absent any court action."

Protesters also continued to voice their objections to the eviction that occurred years earlier, dating back to March 2007, when two reservation residents, Walter Rosales and Karen Toggery, were displaced to make way for the casino. These individuals, with support from JAC, pursued multiple unsuccessful legal avenues in response to the evictions and the demolition of their homes. Although the tribe offered them replacement homes in an alternate location, no compromise was reached.

Penn and the tribe made concerted efforts to publicize their measures to address community concerns. They highlighted several key points, including a 58% reduction in the original height, a 76% reduction in the height visible from the highway, the construction of an underground parking lot, a reduction in the footprint of the casino building, and the selection of earth tones and lighting designed to minimize visual impacts.

While these architectural adjustments incurred significant costs, the most substantial efforts to appease opposition focused on fire safety and roadway improvements. The tribe committed to funding and maintaining a fire station and covering the expenses for major roadway upgrades, including the straightening, and widening of sections of Highway 94.

In a March 2015 press release issued by Penn Gaming, Jamul tribal chairman Raymond Hunter conveyed the tribe's commitment to addressing community concerns:

> "We have worked tirelessly for well over a decade, listening to the voices of the community, addressing concerns, and ultimately developing a project that blends seamlessly into the region while creating approximately 2,500 much-needed construction and permanent jobs in our region. We look forward to continuing to be a good neighbor, as well as becoming a philanthropic leader and an active business partner in San Diego County."

Simultaneously, the tribe had been actively engaging with the local business community in East County, seeking opportunities for partnerships. They expressed their aspiration to turn Chairman Hunter's "long-awaited dream" into a reality, one that would contribute to the prosperity of the entire area. By the spring of 2016, as construction entered its final stages, it became increasingly evident that the casino would finally open its doors.

Jacob's Last Stand

In August 2016, several critical developments occurred. On August 3, Chairwoman Erica M. Pinto, alongside Governor Jerry Brown, signed their next compact ahead of the casino's opening. This new agreement replaced the outdated original compact, which had been burdened by a substantial accumulated debt of $450 million. Subsequently, Supervisor Jacob's office became highly active. On August 15, Jacob sent strongly worded letters to two state agencies.

In her letter to the State Department of Alcoholic Beverage Control, Jacob accused the agency of

> "allowing the casino to serve alcohol prior to the completion of all road improvements and without conducting a public hearing on the liquor permit. This was concerning, especially considering the nearly 100 DUI-related collisions that had occurred on the highway in the past decade. Jacob pointed out that other Indian casinos, such as Sycuan and Barona, had

> taken many years to obtain liquor licenses, whereas the Jamul casino received one in less than 12 months."

On the same day, August 15, 2016, Jacob wrote an even more impassioned letter to Laurie Berman, Director of CalTrans District 11. In this letter, she accused Berman of creating a severe public safety hazard. Furthermore, on that day, The San Diego Union Tribune published an op-ed by Jacob titled "Jamul casino is gambling with public safety." In her op-ed, Jacob criticized the casino's portrayal as a glamorous Las Vegas-style venue, emphasizing that Jamul was a rural community that had fought to maintain its rural character for decades.

Jacob assigned blame for the situation to various parties. She faulted the tribe for not relocating to another reservation and opting to share a casino with another tribe. "Can you imagine your neighbor telling you they don't like you and you should move away to another neighborhood and share a house owned by another family? Who does that?" said Carlene Chamberlain. Penn was criticized for trying to embellish the casino's image while prioritizing financial gains over the community's well-being. Jacob reserved her most significant criticism for CalTrans, accusing the agency of failing in its primary responsibility — protecting the public.

Jacob envisioned a giant catastrophe and convinced some in the community it was coming with the Jamul Casino:

> "Here's the nightmare scenario I worry about most: A big wildfire breaks out in our backcountry and, with the Santa Ana winds, aggressively pushes west. At the same time, a collision occurs on this rural highway. SR-94 turns into a parking lot. Residents can't escape. Folks in the casino's gaming halls and bars can't get out. I'm not talking about a Hollywood movie. I'm talking about a real "Perfect Storm." This casino represents a clear and present danger to the community. State officials need to step up, do their job and put public safety first."

The next day, on August 19, 2016, Jacob and many Jamul residents gathered on a hillside looking down on the soon-to-open Jamul casino. The Supervisor protested "the mammoth development" and again called on state officials to immediately address the public safety hazards posed by the project. While this was to be the last major public event fielded by Jacob and JAC, the legal attack continued. A lawsuit was filed on October 10, 2016, against the Alcoholic Beverages Control Board in a last-ditch effort to stop the casino's liquor license application. Like all the other suits, the JAC maintained its perfect record of failure.

Building Bridges, Keeping Faith

After more than two decades of relentless struggle, Hollywood Casino Jamul finally opened its doors for business on October 10, 2016. The casino boasted a three-story gaming and entertainment facility spanning approximately 200,000 square feet. Inside, visitors could find over 1,700 slot machines, 40 live table games, multiple dining options, bars, lounges, and an underground parking structure with around 1,800 spaces. Notably, it marked the last casino opening in San Diego County, and no other tribe attempting to establish a casino in the country had endured such an arduous journey. The agreement with the county imposed a substantial cost on the tribe, exceeding $10 million annually, with over $300 million designated for road improvements, the fire department, and safety initiatives.

In May 2018, the Penn National Gaming Corp., which owned the Hollywood casinos chain comprising 27 gambling properties, disassociated the casino from its brand and handed over its management to the Jamul Indian Village Development Corporation. Consequently, it was re-branded as the Jamul Casino and is now operated and managed by the Jamul Indian Village of California.

Throughout its protracted battle with Supervisor Jacob, JAC, and CalTrans, the tribe recognized the significance of an effective public outreach program. They conducted numerous public meetings, participated in numerous Rural Fire Protection District (RFPD) board and local planning group meetings, responded to countless letters, collaborated with a team of seasoned consultants, and conducted thorough environmental studies. These efforts aimed to ensure that the public had ample opportunities and time to provide feedback on the project.

The tribe remained committed to its outreach initiatives, with the primary goal being to establish Jamul Indian Village as a responsible and beneficial contributor to the regional economy. As part of this strategy, the tribe placed advertisements in the local monthly publication, the Jamul Shopper. These ads covered topics such as fire safety, a prominent concern in San Diego County's backcountry, and provided helpful editorial commentary on various community issues. Unfortunately, the management of the Jamul Shopper decided to prevent the tribe from placing ads in their publication, effectively discontinuing all future ads from the tribe to the detriment of the Jamul community.

The tribe's outreach endeavors also encompassed numerous meetings with elected officials at the local, state, and federal levels to provide them with the most up-to-date information. Collaborations were initiated with entities such as the RFPD, San Diego County Sheriff's Department, California Highway Patrol, and Caltrans to explore measures for enhancing overall fire safety, law enforcement, and traffic safety in the region.

Through these discussions and outreach initiatives, tribal representatives recognized that many of these government agencies lacked an understanding of tribal governance or its legal and constitutional status in relation to local and state agencies. This realization marked the beginning of a sustained effort to engage with each agency, secure recognition of Jamul Indian Village as a tribal government, and establish government-to-government relations, fostering a dialogue on shared concerns.

A Childhood Tradition:

Racing to the Full Moon

When the moon was full and shined brightly in the sky, the Kumeyaay children would race. One Kumeyaay legend reads that the first boy who sees a full moon is responsible for gathering others so that they could race. The children would race to a spot like a stream or lake and jump in. Because of the moon's reflection on the water, it was as though the children were racing to the moon.

Kumeyaay name for moon for different months:

Halamrtinya	January
Halanitca	February
Halakwol	March
Halanyimcep	April
Halatai	May
Halapisu	June
Halamrtinya	July
Halanitca	August
Halakwol	September

(Start of Kumeyaay year)

Halanyimcep	October
Halatai	November
Halapisu	December

Concerning the fire safety issue, the tribe committed to a $22 million mitigation package for the county. This package included the construction of a $2.5 million to $3 million fire station, $2 million worth of state-of-the-art equipment, and an annual allocation of $900,000 for staffing (including the hiring of additional firefighters) and training.

Well before the casino's opening, the tribe sought to educate its neighbors about its own history. In October 2000, the tribe introduced a traveling exhibit titled "Bringing the Past to Life." The primary objective was to convey their culture to non-Indigenous people and ensure its preservation for future generations. This was achieved through the development of an exhibit that documented the history and contemporary achievements of the Kumeyaay people. Each 26-by-42-inch panel served as an educational tool for schools, complementing their curriculum on indigenous history and local cultures. The exhibit covered various aspects of tribal culture, including ceremonies, legends, food gathering practices, and art forms. This educational initiative was highly effective, with over 10,000 students, educators, and parents in the San Diego area having the opportunity to view the exhibit. For many, this exhibit served as their initial exposure to the history and culture of the indigenous people of the region.

Additionally, alongside the historical panels, the tribe developed a CD-ROM version of the exhibit and a supplementary workbook designed for classroom use. These resources aided teachers in helping students understand the significant contributions made by Native Americans to the region and the state of California. Schools also had the option to arrange presentations by the tribal chair or an elder, who could deliver insights into the tribe's history and culture directly to students.

The Chairwoman at this time, Erica M. Pinto, the first female to be elected as the tribal leader and who was just recently re-elected to another four-year term, has given great additional emphasis to the educational mission. On November 5th, 2019, she wrote to Governor Newsom as follows:

> In April this year, San Diego celebrated the landing in 1769 of the first contingent of Spanish settlers and the 'founding' of San Diego. To the Kumeyaay people, that landing was a catastrophe marking the end of our freedom. When I was invited to attend the 'celebration,' I decided to use the occasion to tell my fellow San Diegans some of the truth about the Spaniards' gross mistreatment of my ancestors. I did so respectfully and ended by urging that we begin an honest dialogue that could lead to true reconciliation.
>
> It was clear to me that many of the people who heard my remarks were either genuinely puzzled or offended. They were hearing — literally for the first time — some deeply unpalatable historical truths.
>
> I do not doubt the goodwill of most of my fellow citizens: if they knew the true history of California, they would understand and support the need for truth telling and reconciliation. The fundamental problem is that they were taught from school textbooks that celebrated conquest.
>
> I recognize the enormous difficulties of re-writing school history textbooks. Yet, I believe you — and only you — have the moral authority to jump-start that process. Most respectfully, I urge you to do so.
>
> In 50 years', time, San Diego will celebrate its tercentenary. My hope is that by then all its citizens will know the true history of the land on which they live.

The Bedrock of Sovereignty, Land into Trust

The bedrock of tribal sovereignty hinges on securing land into trust, creating a dedicated jurisdiction for tribal governance. The Jamul Indian Village faced a unique challenge: they were granted six acres, one of the smallest reservations in the nation. To put this into perspective, consider the Navajo Nation, with a sprawling 17,574,000 acres of trust land. Clearly, the Jamul tribe's land isn't suited for agriculture.

The process of obtaining land into trust is governed by the Bureau of Indian Affairs, seemingly straightforward on paper but inherently political in practice. This often-protracted process can stretch from three to eight years, or even longer. The Jamul Indian Village initiated its quest for land into trust in 2002, submitting various parcels for housing, healthcare facilities, and mixed-use commercial space to bolster their economy.

Chairman Leon Acebedo led the tribe through this complex process, which required multiple trips to Washington D.C. to advocate for their land into trust applications.

> *"It was a long and difficult battle. Even at one time afterwards, I met personally with a former employee of the Bureau of Indian Affairs who actually was responsible for evaluating our application for land into trust, Mr. George Skibine at a dinner meeting he indicated to me after he asked about the status of our application, he told me there was no reason why our application should not have been approved at that time."*
>
> Chairman Leon Acebedo

Astonishingly, as of 2021, they still await a response to their long-standing application.

SHINGLE SPRINGS BAND OF MIWOK INDIANS
EL DORADO COUNTY

CHAPTER FIVE

The Shingle Springs Band of Miwok Indians

The major participants in this case are:

The Shingle Springs Band

For centuries, the Maidu and Miwok people, native to Northeastern Central California, lived in small bands that were geographically dispersed among the valleys, foothills, and mountains of the region. There was occasional intermarriage with other Indians and in the late 19th century even with Hawaiians who were brought into the area as laborers.

The Nisenan or Southern Maidu, who were among the ancestors of the Indians we know today as the Shingle Springs Band of Miwok Indians, occupied the whole of the American, Bear, and Yuba River drainages. Hunter-gatherers, these Indians were known as cultivators of tobacco, weavers of extremely fine baskets, and responsible for the spread of California's Black Oak forests (which they harvested for acorns).

The Maidu and Miwok tribes, native to Northeastern Central California, signed treaties with the United States in 1852. These 18 treaties, known as 'The Barbour Treaties,' were meant to establish reservations for these tribes. What happened to them? Why weren't they ratified? The government claims they were forgotten and went un-ratified for half a century. It wasn't until 1905 that the U.S. Senate rediscovered these treaties and officially recognized the injustice. The response was to buy land for 'landless Indians' in California and encourage them to live on 'rancherias,' which were small reservations.

The Shingle Springs Rancheria had its beginnings in 1916 when the government purchased an 80-acre parcel known as the 'El Dorado' tract. This land was intended for landless Indians in the El Dorado County area. In 1920, an additional 160-acre parcel known as the 'Verona Tract' was acquired. The deed for this land stated its purpose as "the use and occupancy of the Sacramento-Verona Band of Homeless Indians."

Several decades later, the State of California and CalTrans began planning the construction and expansion of Highway 50. Without consulting the tribe, they decided in 1960 to build the highway through and over the El Dorado Tract. Given the history between tribes and the State of California it was no surprise that they made no acknowledgment of the existence of a tribal government or tribal families on this land.

Despite pleas to the Bureau of Indian Affairs (BIA), the trust status of the El Dorado Tract was revoked. This allowed CalTrans to use 28 acres, originally designated as tribal land, for the highway. The remaining 52 acres were sold to private owners. In 1965, Highway 50 was constructed, cutting through the only access route to the reservation - the Verona Tract. As a result, the local Indians lost a third of their rancheria's land and were left with no practical access to the remaining territory, effectively becoming a landlocked island.

In the late 1970s, members of the Verona Band of Homeless Indians took steps to organize and comply with the Indian Reorganization Act. Their Articles of Association were approved on December 10, 1976, and they became known as the Shingle Springs Band of Miwok Indians. Despite having around 500 tribal members, only a few lived on their landlocked rancheria due to a lack of housing and resources.

The Shingle Springs Tribal Council during this time included Chairman Nick Fonseca and Councilmembers Elaine Whitehurst, Louie Adams, Beth Ann Bodi, Annie Jones, Stephanie Cuellar, Rose Campbell and Jim Adams.

The Homeowners Association

The Miwok tribe needed a formal way to access their reservation for tribal members who wanted to live there. Additionally, if they wanted to pursue economic development on their land, having proper access was crucial. After exploring various options, they initially found only one viable solution: negotiating a right of way on a private road through a neighboring residential development.

This agreement was made with an upscale private neighborhood called the Grassy Run Subdivision. It was essentially a homeowner association (HOA), a legal entity formed for managing and maintaining the private road within the community. In California, such associations are recognized by law and are often established by developers during the creation and sale of residential properties. Grassy Run was home to predominantly white middle- and upper-class residents who intentionally chose a rural living environment, with large parcels and a private road that they controlled.

El Dorado County

El Dorado County, located in the Sierra Nevada region and known for its gold mining history, is predominantly rural with hilly and mountainous terrain. It encompasses part of Lake Tahoe and Folsom Lake, with more than half of its land being public, including the vast Eldorado National Forest and the popular Desolation Wilderness for outdoor activities.

In the year 2000, the county had a total population of 156,000, with the majority (89%) being Caucasian, and only a small percentage (1%) identified as Native Americans (specifically, Maidu, Miwuk, and Washoe Indians). The per capita income was $25,560, and the median household income stood at $51,484, which was relatively low compared to other counties in California. The more affluent communities were Placerville (population 11,000) and South Lake Tahoe (population 22,000).

El Dorado County is governed by a five-member Board of Supervisors, with most of the population residing in unincorporated areas, giving the board significant authority. The elected Sheriff holds a crucial role in administration and politics, as only Placerville and South Lake Tahoe have their own police departments. Large landowners have historically had a notable influence on county politics.

Politically, El Dorado County has consistently supported Republican candidates in presidential and congressional elections since 1976, making it one of the most socially conservative areas in California. Tom McClintock, who represents a significant portion of the county, is known as one of the state's most conservative members in Congress.

El Dorado County LAFCO

Since 1963, California counties have established Local Area Formation Commissions (LAFCOs) to manage regulatory and planning responsibilities. LAFCO's primary goal is to address community needs, including development, by overseeing the creation, expansion, governance, and dissolution of local government agencies and their service areas. One significant task of LAFCOs is to define "spheres of influence" or growth boundaries that outline expected future service areas. While LAFCOs typically act in response to petitions from local entities, landowners, or registered voters, they also have the authority to initiate proposals themselves.

El Dorado County's LAFCO consists of seven regular Commissioners, including two from the Board of Supervisors, two representing cities, two representing special districts, and one member selected from the public by the other Commissioners. Additionally, there are four alternate Commissioners, one from each of the first three membership categories. The Executive Director of LAFCO holds considerable influence and is often an individual with planning expertise. It's important to note that El Dorado's LAFCO has never officially recognized the Shingle Springs Band of Miwok Indians Tribal Government, consequently excluding tribal participation in the commission's planning and proceedings.

Stand Up for California!

In the early 2000s, there was a nationwide backlash against Indian gaming, which gained attention through a series of Time Magazine articles with titles like "Wheel of Misfortune," "Who Gets the Money?" and "Playing the Political Slots." These articles raised several critical allegations against tribal casinos, including claims that their profits benefitted external investors, they exacerbated issues related to gambling addiction, were poor neighbors to the affected communities, and made limited contributions to improving the overall well-being of the majority of Native Americans.

In the resistance against California's tribal casinos, several groups like 'United Property Owners,' which operated out of Washington State, and the 'California Coalition Against Gambling Expansion' had some brief prominence. In this historical context and in the majority of conflicts surrounding the establishment of new casinos in California, the foremost leader of opposition was 'Stand Up For California!' (SUFC). Remarkably, even today, SUFC continues to exert significant influence in the state's anti-gaming landscape.

SUFC is officially registered as a non-profit, public service corporation with the California Secretary of State. According to their mission statement, SUFC's objectives are two-fold:

1. To educate lawmakers, law enforcement, local governments, and citizens about the cultural, economic, and political implications of state and tribal government gaming.

2. To formulate a targeted policy framework that ensures the protection of communities, local governments, and tribal

> governments, while fostering mutually cooperative and beneficial government-to-government relationships.

Despite presenting itself as a 'statewide organization,' SUFC was essentially a solo endeavor, managed from a spare room on a small ranch. Its operations were overseen by Cheryl Schmit, a former soccer mom and grade school librarian. A 2003 Los Angeles Times article titled "In Casino Wars, She's a Player" detailed how Cheryl Schmit rose to prominence as a formidable opponent of California's tribal gaming industry. In 1996, when a tribe proposed constructing a casino merely a mile from her two-acre ranch near Penryn in Yolo County, Schmit rallied her neighbors and successfully persuaded the tribe to choose an alternative location far from Penryn.

Cheryl Schmit, often described as an 'accidental activist,' inadvertently transformed herself into a full-time advocate against California's tribal gaming industry. The Los Angeles Times characterized her as the go-to figure for opposing Indian casinos in the state, a one-woman force taking on the formidable $5-billion tribal gambling industry. While her supporters affectionately dubbed her a 'velvet pit bull,' many Native American tribes viewed her as the 'Wicked Witch of the West.'

The Case History

In rural California, few issues can strain neighborly relations as much as the maintenance of country roads, which are susceptible to storm damage, winter ruts, and the need for regular resurfacing, often on an annual basis. Complications arose in a particular case involving a private road initially constructed exclusively for the use of the original homeowners in a neighborhood. These homeowners began to resent their "new" neighbors, who were members of the Shingle Springs Tribe, even though tribal members had been living in the area long before the new housing development and the establishment of the so-called "private" community.

"With no real access to our reservation, we had no choice but to fight and to continue finding a long-term solution that would allow our tribe uninterrupted access to our reservation. After all, without access and the ability to build houses and conduct tribal business, we have no real sovereignty," said Chairman Nicholas Fonseca.

Initially, after the agreement was reached, there were minimal conflicts between the tribe and the Homeowners Association (HOA) regarding the right of way. Tensions started to rise as tribal traffic on the road increased due to the development of housing for tribal members and the tribe's plans for potential casino and other economic ventures. At this point, emotions began to run high, with few Grassy Run residents aware or concerned about the fact that Shingle Springs Tribe members had been residing in the area for decades before the inception of the Grassy Run development.

The residents of Grassy Run were not only annoyed by the increased traffic in their community due to the tribe but were also concerned about the potential for even more significant traffic if a casino were to be constructed. Homeowners in the area were unified in their opposition and were determined to make life difficult for tribal members and anyone else using the private road to access the reservation.

Many tribal members were eager to return and live on the reservation, but the housing shortage was a major obstacle preventing them from doing so. The tribe's primary focus during this period was to create housing opportunities for those members who wanted to return to the reservation.

To address this housing need, tribal members invested in mobile homes, which had to be transported to the reservation in sections using 18-wheel trucks with long trailers. This process required meticulous planning, substantial time, and expenses for tribal members. Assembling the homes on the reservation was necessary, and it provided an opportunity for the HOA to obstruct the tribe's plans.

Along the road leading to the reservation, there was a single-lane bridge that all vehicles had to use when traveling to and from the reservation. Vehicles had to stop at the bridge, allowing only one vehicle at a time to cross. The HOA claimed that the installation of safety rails on the bridge was intended to enhance safety by preventing vehicles from driving off the bridge into the stream below.

Initially, the new safety rails on the bridge appeared to be typical safety features; however, it became very clear they were deliberately designed to obstruct the tribal members. Recognizing that tribal members used 18-wheel vehicles to transport mobile homes on the private road, the HOA installed side rails that were 14 inches taller than usual, blocking the necessary clearances for these large vehicles. This was a deliberate attempt to prevent tribal members from transporting homes to the reservation and settling there.

In response to what they viewed as a dirty trick by the HOA, the tribe drew upon their ancestral craftsmanship and skills. Louie Adams, Jim Adams, Nick Fonseca and a group of tribal members came together and created a smaller, narrow bridge that could be placed in the middle of the road to raise the 18-wheel vehicles approximately 20 inches above the ground, providing the required clearance. The construction of this makeshift bridge involved about 20 individuals and took around two months to design, build, and make it portable for easy setup and removal once a home was transported across.

While some might have considered giving up or resorting to violence, the Shingle Springs tribe found a peaceful and practical solution. Chairman Nicholas Fonseca emphasized their determination, stating, "We will not be stopped from bringing housing for our tribal members." Despite the bridge-on-the-bridge solution, it remained a significant endeavor, requiring 20 to 30 people to assemble it and guide the trucks across, given that each home consisted of two to three pieces.

The tribe's innovative approach further fueled the anger of the HOA residents. In response, the HOA attempted to restrict the tribe by imposing time limits on their road usage and declared that blocking the bridge for any reason was a public safety concern. They introduced new regulations stipulating that the tribe could not block the bridge

for more than 90 minutes within any 24-hour period. Undeterred, the tribe devised a strategy to place the bridge, position the 18-wheeler near it, and get one trailer across the bridge within the 90-minute deadline. While this approach allowed them to transport homes, it extended the time required to bring a home to the reservation from one day to three days.

Despite numerous efforts by homeowners to impede the housing initiatives, the tribe remained resolute in their determination to bring homes to the reservation. Tribal members pooled their resources and invested approximately $40,000 to design and construct the bridge.

This undertaking represented a substantial financial commitment and time investment, involving the labor of 20 to 30 tribal members for each crossing, given the time restrictions imposed by the HOA. It also resulted in lost income for the tribe. Nonetheless, they deemed it a worthwhile expense to enable tribal members to return home.

The homeowners, with a mix of disdain and begrudging recognition of the tribe's determination, looked on as the tribe set up and removed the bridge daily to transport single sections of houses. Eventually, the HOA leadership, realizing that nothing they did would deter the tribe from accessing their reservation, agreed to a ceasefire. This entailed the installation of removable rails, permitting the tribe to take down the rails according to a scheduled plan to transport their homes across. This agreement marked the conclusion of this phase in the ongoing struggle with the homeowners. The homeowners, however, were not finished with their efforts to stop the tribe.

"People often asked us why did you put up with the homeowner's association and all of their games? It's quite simple, our people deserve housing on the reservation; it's about a better quality of life," said Councilmember Louie Adams.

Nevertheless, the tribe had gleaned an important lesson from the protracted battle: they needed to identify an alternative access point to the reservation. They began exploring various options with potential investors to secure access, eventually concluding that the most effective means of guaranteeing access to their reservation was to fund and construct an off-ramp from Highway 50 themselves.

As tensions between the tribe and the HOA escalated, the HOA decided to establish a special district with the primary purpose of overseeing the repair, maintenance, and enhancement of the Grassy Run Road. This new special district, named the Grassy Run Community Services District (GRCSD), was established by the Eldorado County Local Area Formation Commission. It was situated midway between the Shingle Springs and Diamond Springs communities, positioned north of Highway 50. The formation of GRCSD subsequently became the focal point of conflict between the tribe and the community. This situation was highly volatile and had its roots in CalTrans' decision to collaborate with the tribe in constructing an off-ramp from Highway 50 on the rancheria's land.

In 1994, Governor Pete Wilson, a vocal opponent of tribal gaming, secured his reelection for a second term. Nevertheless, certain California tribes, confident in their tribal sovereignty and inspired by the remarkable success of gaming tribes on the East Coast, moved forward with plans to establish casinos on tribal lands, irrespective of state laws. One such tribe was the Yocha Dehe Wintun Nation, also known as the Rumsey Band of Indians.

The Rumsey Band aimed to open a casino in Penryn, located in Yolo County. In this quiet corner of eastern Yolo County, they encountered formidable opposition from Cheryl Schmit. She effectively organized opposition against the tribe and their investors, rallying her neighbors, generating resistance among local officials, and launching an aggressive public relations campaign in the local media. Ultimately, she compelled the tribe to relocate their plans to Cache Creek in western Yolo County, which was a full hour's journey away from Penryn. This victory was a significant achievement and news of it quickly spread to neighboring El Dorado County and throughout the state.

The Big Tent Casino

Much like the Rumsey Rancheria Indians, the Shingle Springs Rancheria saw a casino as a means of economic development, believing it would bolster their sovereignty and provide tribal members with improved prospects. In early 1995, discussions within the tribe revolved around the prospect of opening a casino. The tribe's strategic location, with Highway 50 passing near their property, appeared to offer an opportunity to tap into the gambling market in the broader Sacramento area and potentially attract gamblers en route to Reno and Lake Tahoe. Drawing inspiration from southern California tribes using tents for housing Bingo games and video slot machines, tribal leaders engaged in discussions with gaming entrepreneur Chris Anderson, who operated the company Sharp Image, based outside Chatsworth in Los Angeles County. Sharp Image specialized in the sale and leasing of video slot machines, as the experiences of East Coast gaming tribes had demonstrated the profitability of slots, and Anderson aimed to capitalize on California's growing gaming market.

In late 1995, Anderson negotiated with Nicholas Fonseca and the Shingle Springs Rancheria leadership to establish agreements. He sought an exclusive right to construct their casino and furnish it with machines and tables, with plans to build the tent and invest the necessary funds. On May 24, 1996, the tribe and Sharp Image formalized a 'Gaming Machine Agreement.' Concurrently, preparations were already underway for a concrete pad to serve as the foundation for a 20,000 square-foot tent housing 400 slot machines. Construction activities, including the transportation of cement by large trucks along their private road, exacerbated the frustrations of Grassy Run homeowners to a boiling point.

Some homeowners were so incensed that they engaged in direct action to halt the traffic, deploying tire chains and devices to puncture the tires of incoming trucks and cars. One homeowner, who had been videotaping the incoming traffic, accidentally left his video recorder on the ground, still recording, as he went to assist with setting up the chains. Upon discovering the camera, the tribe found footage not only of the chain placement but also images of the owner and others throwing rocks at passing vehicles. As a result, not only this homeowner but several others were arrested, and the FBI was called in to assist with their prosecution.

Homeowners were aware of Cheryl Schmit's battle against the casino in Yolo County, given her ranch's proximity to Grassy Run, just 35 miles away. She provided them with guidance and advice. Furthermore, the El Dorado County Supervisors and the County Sheriff maintained communication with their counterparts in Yolo County. The homeowners prepared legal action in the local Superior

Court, and both sides retained legal counsel. The stage was set for a showdown between the tribe and the local community, a genuine test of popular sovereignty versus tribal sovereignty.

Battling for Control of the Arena

The lawsuits and community opposition against the planned casino didn't escape the attention of the Bureau of Indian Affairs (BIA) or the National Indian Gaming Commission (NIGC). In fact, the County, Stand Up For California (SUFC), and the Homeowners' Association (HOA) worked diligently to raise their concerns with officials in both federal agencies and the media.

Initially, on August 6, 1996, the NIGC approved the tribe's proposed gaming ordinance. This approval was seen as a minor victory, as the ordinance had been carefully modeled after ordinances from other tribes that had already gained agency approval. Following this, the NIGC dispatched field officers from its Enforcement Division with the task of attending local government hearings and reporting on the community's concerns.

In El Dorado County, public meetings were convened, bringing together representatives from the NIGC, BIA, the County, all the opposing community groups, and the small minority of local supporters of the tribe who were willing to voice their opinions. The NIGC field officer relayed to the headquarters that the primary concerns revolved around environmental issues, public health, and safety, particularly during fire emergencies. It's likely that the officer, informally, also conveyed the depth of community opposition, given the strong reactions of locals who participated in these meetings.

In response, the tribe agreed to collaborate with the NIGC and committed not to open the gaming facility until the identified concerns were addressed. The NIGC then entered a contract with Parallax Incorporated to assess the proposed casino's environmental, health, and safety aspects. On October 4, 1996, the NIGC furnished the tribe with a report from Parallax, titled "Preliminary Environmental, Health, and Safety Assessment." This report highlighted several serious issues and offered recommendations for mitigation.

While the tribe perceived the assessment as unfair, they engaged with NIGC personnel to determine the necessary steps for implementing the recommendations. Both parties agreed on a process through which the NIGC could verify that the required corrective actions had been taken. As part of NIGC's procedural requirements, additional hearings with local government representatives and community members were conducted. In a letter of October 21, 1996, the tribe informed the NIGC of its intentions to advertise and conduct a public hearing.

The hearing, held on October 26, featured presentations from the County, Grassy Run Community Services District (GCSD), and community groups, all expressing their concerns that significant environmental, health, and safety issues remained unresolved. Sensing that the opposition was deeply rooted, the tribe held internal meetings to discuss the situation and unanimously decided that it was in the tribe's best interest to proceed with the gaming facility's operation, to be named the Crystal Mountain Casino. They communicated this decision to the NIGC through a 14-page letter dated October 30.

The tribe inaugurated its 'Big Tent' on November 2, 1996, marking the opening of the Crystal Mountain Casino. As part of its launch, the casino hosted the monthly meeting of CNIGA, the statewide association of tribes, at their new facility. These gatherings provided a platform for tribes across the state to discuss tribal matters, politics, and upcoming challenges. I attended these monthly meetings and can attest that, on this occasion, the first CNIGA visitors faced a hostile reception. Residents from the HOA threw rocks and other objects at cars as they entered the road to the reservation and casino. It was a trying and even perilous time, as the vehicles' windows and windshields were damaged by the projectiles. Similar attacks were directed at the initial patrons of the casino.

In response to the tribe's casino opening, the NIGC issued a 'Notice of Violation' (NOV) on November 5. The allegation was that the tribe had failed to implement a substantial number of the Parallax recommendations, particularly those related to fire safety and water issues. Reluctantly accepting this judgment, the tribe voluntarily closed Crystal Mountain Casino on November 11.

The demise of Crystal Mountain Casino resulted from a convergence of local community activism and bureaucratic opposition from the NIGC. It would never reopen.

It appears that neither the tribe nor Anderson fully grasped the permanence of the casino closure. On November 15th, 1997, the tribe entered both an 'Equipment Loan Agreement' and a 'Promissory Note.' Were these agreements legally binding and enforceable under California law? Most likely, they were. A question that neither party seemed to consider was the implications of federal law. What legal recourse would Anderson have if, as indeed happened in 1999, the tribe decided to terminate its machine lease agreement with Sharp Image? And how would tribal sovereignty factor into this dispute, if at all? In many instances, tribal sovereignty can supersede contracts with non-tribal entities or individuals, unless there's a waiver of sovereign immunity.

The Tribe, NIGC and the Private Road

The tribe and its legal representatives maintained an ongoing dialogue with the NIGC chair and enforcement officials to resolve the issues outlined in the NOV. On February 20, 1997, the tribe formally appealed the NOV and followed up with a 'Supplemental Statement' dated February 28, asserting that they had fully addressed and remedied all the concerns raised in the Notice of Violation.

At this time, the NIGC Chair was Ada Deer, a prominent advocate for Native American rights and a member of the Menominee tribe. She had previously headed the BIA (Bureau of Indian Affairs). Chairwoman Deer responded to the appeal by noting that some problems had not been satisfactorily resolved, and certain remedial actions had not been verified. As a result, she directed NIGC field investigators to conduct another site visit to the casino.

On March 5, the NIGC field investigator, after completing the site visit, acknowledged that some progress had been made and encouraged the tribe to continue working with the Chair and enforcement division officials to address all the issues raised in the NOV. Then, on March 21, Chairwoman Deer issued a ruling stating that the tribe had adequately addressed all identified problems, with one exception: their failure to collaborate with the Diamond Springs Fire District in preparing for a fire emergency and evacuation. In a subsequent telephone conference held in April among the involved parties, she emphasized that the NIGC considered this to be the sole remaining obstacle and urged efforts to resolve it.

Losing in Federal Court

Despite their ongoing issues with the NIGC and the local fire district, the tribe recognized that their economic prospects were contingent upon having road access to their land. In 1996, they initiated a lawsuit against the Grassy Run Community Services District (GRCSD) in the United States District Court in Sacramento. The tribe alleged violations of their constitutional rights and contended that they possessed legally protected rights of access to their rancheria via the Grassy Run roads.

The Grassy Run Homeowners' Association (HOA) intervened in the lawsuit, filing a counterclaim against both the tribe and the County. The HOA asserted that the Grassy Run roads were private and had never been dedicated or intended for public use.

In April 1997, District Court Judge David F. Levi issued a partial summary judgment, determining that the roads were indeed private and had not been dedicated to public use. He encouraged the parties to attempt to resolve their remaining disputes in light of his ruling.

Neither side was inclined to compromise. The homeowners, emboldened by the favorable ruling and aggravated by the escalating legal costs, remained unyielding. The tribe, also burdened by litigation expenses, was frustrated by the federal court's failure to acknowledge their sovereign rights.

Nonetheless, settlement discussions took place between the tribe's chairman, Nicholas Fonseca, and the GRCSD, with attorneys deeply engaged on both sides. These discussions eventually culminated in a 'Settlement Agreement,' contingent upon approval by the GRCSD, the HOA, and the tribal council. While the GRCSD and the HOA endorsed the agreement, the tribal council rejected it. Consequently, Grassy Run sought a court order to prohibit the tribe from using the Grassy Run roads to access the rancheria for purposes other than residential, non-commercial access.

In December 1997, the federal district court issued a preliminary injunction that imposed restrictions on road access, including specified time periods and vehicle size limitations. Permission from the president of the HOA or her representative was mandated for road use, with exceptions granted for rancheria residents and their guests, residential service providers, government officials, periodic tribal government meetings, and occasional educational and cultural events. This ruling constituted a significant setback for the tribe. If it remained in effect, it would effectively derail the tribe's plans for a casino, housing, and any form of economic development on their reservation. Consequently, in early 1999, the tribe appealed this decision to the Ninth Circuit Court of Appeals.

Shortly thereafter, when the tribe terminated its contracts with Sharp Image, relations with Anderson deteriorated due to his insistence on immediate repayment of his investment. To exert influence over the Grassy Run board, Anderson purchased several homes in GCSD. For years, he engaged in an ever-escalating campaign of threats and harassment against the tribe until, as we will discuss later, he filed a lawsuit against the tribe seeking $250 million in damages.

Not a Recognized Government, Caltrans Will Not Talk to You

If the tribe couldn't utilize the private road, they required a connection between the public road, Highway 50, and their rancheria. Initially, they believed they had a strong case against CalTrans for this purpose, as CalTrans had, in fact, caused their access problem when it relocated the Highway in 1965.

The tribe's goal was to secure an off-ramp diverting traffic from Highway 50 onto a new road, which would not only provide access but also lead to the location on the rancheria where they intended to construct the casino. They understood that additional construction might be necessary, such as a bridge, and they were eager to discuss the associated costs and feasibility with CalTrans engineers.

This endeavor proved to be incredibly challenging. CalTrans' senior staff and engineers had no prior experience or interest in collaborating with Indian tribes. They had historically interacted with county or city governments, not individuals or representatives from tribal communities. They seemed either wholly unaware or unwilling to acknowledge that tribes also held governmental status. As a result, they flatly refused to meet with the tribe's leaders or representatives. They cited CalTrans' rules and regulations as not requiring them to engage with tribes or members of the public, asserting that they were only obligated to work with local governments. Their stance essentially amounted to: "If it's not in our manual, we can't do it, and nowhere in our manual does it state that we can or must deal with Native Americans."

Even as late as 1999, when the Governor of California was finalizing a government-to-government compact with the tribe, CalTrans persisted in denying any responsibility to engage with them. Despite the tribe's offer to fully fund the project with financial support from Lakes, CalTrans remained obstinate in their refusal to cooperate.

The situation took on a rather surreal quality as the tribe and its public affairs consultants found themselves in the peculiar position of having to educate CalTrans on federal laws that unequivocally establish federally recognized Indian tribes as sovereign tribal governments. They provided extensive documentation to CalTrans, outlining the historical context of national jurisprudence regarding tribes, the statutory provisions of the Indian Reorganization Act (IRA) and the Indian

Gaming Regulatory Act (IGRA), as well as the tribe's own history of recognition and sovereignty claims. When these educational efforts failed to yield results, the tribe resorted to threats of legal action.

Despite these various attempts, CalTrans remained unyielding in its refusal to meet, and when meetings were scheduled, they were often abruptly canceled. It appeared to be a deliberate and systematic agency-wide policy. The tribe began to suspect that factors beyond mere ignorance of Indian law were at play. Perhaps officials from El Dorado County, who had relations with CalTrans, were exerting influence? Maybe anti-gaming forces, possibly led by Stand Up For California! (SUFC), were operating behind the scenes? Or perhaps other gaming tribes in the Sacramento area were discreetly involved?

In response, the tribe sought to bring their predicament with CalTrans to the attention of California legislators, urging them to compel CalTrans to engage with tribal governments. Many legislators, who had recently approved government-to-government contracts between the state and tribes, were astonished to discover that CalTrans had refused to collaborate with the tribe. After further advocacy and education by the tribe and their consultants, the Legislature passed a bill and sent it to Governor Davis, mandating that CalTrans recognize, meet, and collaborate with tribal governments on transportation matters. This legislative victory would prove to be short-lived for the Shingle Springs Tribe.

It's unclear whether CalTrans resented the legislative pressure or if the Governor was influenced by competing tribes, other gaming interests, or county officials and residents. Regardless, in September 2000, Governor Davis vetoed the bill, citing concerns about the suitability of the Shingle Springs Rancheria for a casino and its impact on the neighborhood, without directly addressing the core issue that a state agency under his jurisdiction had refused to acknowledge and cooperate with a tribal government.

Consequently, the tribe had to embark on a costly lobbying campaign once again. They eventually succeeded in getting Assembly

Bill 1564, authored by Assemblyman Tony Cardenas, through the legislature and signed by the Governor in 2001. This marked a historic moment for California tribes as it was the first time a tribe had managed to change state law to compel a state agency to recognize and collaborate with a tribal government. The efforts of the Shingle Springs Tribe, led by their lobbyist Luisa Sustaita and coordinated by Jose Cornejo, Chief of Staff to Assemblymember Cardenas, paved the way for numerous California tribes to benefit from this legislation in their future discussions and negotiations with state agencies.

Nevertheless, the relationship with CalTrans remained challenging. It took persistent efforts over the following two years, working closely with CalTrans engineers, to outline a feasible project. The agency insisted that the project should encompass more than just a single off-ramp; it needed to involve the construction of a four-lane cloverleaf interchange and bridges. As a result, the tribe's initial cost estimates doubled, and then doubled again as the project evolved.

The final plans for the project necessitated the construction of an interchange, which came at a cost of $45 million, financed through a bond sale by Lakes, the tribe's investor. This interchange was designed to include a striking four-span, post-tensioned, cast-in-place concrete flyover bridge. Traffic from the eastbound on-ramp would pass beneath two single-span bridges carrying both eastbound and westbound Highway 50 traffic through the interchange. Additionally, westbound on- and off-ramps were part of the overall facility.

The sheer scale of this planned project becomes apparent when considering the physical requirements involved. This encompassed the movement of approximately 170,000 cubic yards of earth, the use of around 35,000 tons of asphalt concrete for paving the ramps and overlaying Highway 50, and the utilization of some 8,500 cubic yards of structural concrete for constructing the bridges and retaining walls. A project of this magnitude not only necessitates the preparation of an intricately detailed 'Environmental Document' but also frequently becomes a target for opposing groups and legal challenges.

Indeed, the adequacy of the Environmental Document prepared by CalTrans was swiftly challenged in the Superior Court. El Dorado County, supported by local community groups, contested the entire document, covering aspects such as traffic, biological resources, air quality, noise and vibration, visual resources, cultural resources, hazardous materials, and drainage. The court's ruling mandated that CalTrans develop comprehensive mitigation measures in each of these categories. This outcome marked a clear setback for the tribe. It took two years before the agency published its Final Supplemental Environmental Impact Report to address the concerns raised by the court. Ultimately, more than a decade after the tribe's initial engagement with CalTrans, groundbreaking activities commenced for the project.

More Lawsuits and the Outline of a Deal

As the 20th century ended, the El Dorado County Supervisors could look back on a series of successful actions in opposition to the tribe's casino plans. The residents of Grassy Run had effectively prevented the tribe's commercial traffic from using the road, backed by a legal determination that the road was indeed private, thus leaving the tribe's reservation inaccessible to casino and commercial traffic. Public sentiment, largely influenced by figures like Cheryl Schmit and other anti-gaming advocates, had turned decisively against the tribe. Additionally, the supervisors were likely aware of the deteriorating relationship between the tribe and its initial investor, Anderson, who was threatening legal action to recover his investment. Furthermore, they might have learned of the tribe's negotiations with potential new investors in 1998.

At this juncture, it appears that the County established contact with Schmit and SUFC. In her initial foray into statewide anti-gaming politics in 1998, Schmit had accused "fundamentalist tribal leaders" of using gambling profits to exert control over California's public policies and seize private property. Her approach shifted towards pragmatism after 1999, with her main objective being the limitation of Indian gaming expansion. She particularly targeted "reservation shopping" by tribes relocating to areas without ancestral ties, and she sought to compel tribes to reimburse local communities for expenses related to police and fire protection, road maintenance, and other costs stemming from the casinos. This stance aligned with the viewpoints of some El Dorado County supervisors.

Schmit stated that her focus was on "the fallout," meaning the effects of casino developments on the environment, government services, traffic, and community character. Central to her campaigns was the belief that the property rights of California property owners were being infringed upon by federal and state policies favoring Indian tribes at the expense of local communities.

Gaming tribes contended that Schmit was not merely a volunteer activist but a paid consultant representing competing interests. They alleged that she had connections to card clubs, Nevada gambling interests, and a hostile union, and they accused her of maintaining a secret alliance with Howard Dickstein, a prominent attorney representing tribes that chose a different path. They further accused her of employing underhanded tactics, promoting violence and racism, and creating chaos and diversions to facilitate lawsuits and delay tribal gaming projects.

While there is no official record of what the County's General Counsel was advising the Board during this period, it's plausible that there were concerns that the Ninth Circuit of Appeals might overturn the District Court's 1997 ruling. The Supervisors were likely aware that the Rumsey Band had agreed to substantial payments to Yolo County in exchange for permission to construct their Cache Creek casino. Moreover, it's certain, as evidenced by media campaigns and SUFC newsletters, that the Supervisors were aware that the Shingle Springs Rancheria was one of the 57 tribes negotiating compacts in Sacramento. After the approval of the tribe's compact in the early 2000s, at least some of the Supervisors, though not necessarily the representative of the supervisorial district encompassing the Shingle

Springs Rancheria, began to contemplate the benefits of a deal with the tribe. After all, there were still numerous county projects requiring funding, and the casino held the potential to generate revenue for investment in local initiatives.

Not all media coverage of SUFC during this period was favorable. The Time investigation uncovered some financial connections that raised questions. For instance, Schmit had received a $20,000 donation from Nevada interests and a $10,000 contribution from the Hotel Employees and Restaurant Employees Union (HERE), which was looking to unionize casino employees. Additionally, she admitted to working as a $4,500-a-month consultant for a coalition of Los Angeles County cities with card clubs that were losing business to tribal casinos. Schmit maintained that her relationship with Howard Dickstein was strictly professional and uncompensated. Howard Dickstein, a well-known attorney, had been a controversial figure within the gaming tribe's community due to his involvement in crafting revenue-sharing agreements for his tribal clients. These agreements were contentious because they required tribes to share a portion of their gaming profits with local municipalities, which some believed threatened the financial sovereignty of the tribes.

The Time's article concluded on a positive note. The reporter seemed to attribute SUFC's accomplishments primarily to Schmit's leadership, organizational skills, and the dedication of fellow volunteers. Addressing allegations of racism and inappropriate behavior, the article cited friends who dismissed these claims, asserting that Schmit actively distanced herself from violence and aggressive tactics. It highlighted the fact that in 1998, Schmit had severed ties with a SUFC leader in neighboring El Dorado County who had been arrested for laying down chains and throwing nails on the road to block access to the Shingle Springs planned tribal casino.

In the early 2000s, the County took legal action as one of its initial moves in the new century. As previously discussed, they filed a lawsuit against Caltrans in state court, alleging violations of the California

Environmental Quality Act (CEQA) concerning the approved interchange. The County argued that the interchange would overload Highway 50's traffic capacity and that inadequate assessments of pollution and other environmental impacts had been conducted.

Upon learning of the BIA and NIGC's approval of the tribe's 'Development and Management Agreement' with Lakes Entertainment and Kean-Argovitz, the County challenged this in federal court. The County contended that the federal agencies had downplayed or disregarded the severe environmental consequences of the casino and had failed to impose substantial mitigation measures.

A second claim, consistent with tactics used by opponents of Indian gaming, was that the tribe lacked legal recognition under federal law. This argument, based on BIA records, asserted that the tribe had no historical claim to its reservation. It claimed that "two unrelated groups of Indians" from Sutter and Sacramento Counties had never historically operated as a tribe, lacked a historical relationship with El Dorado County, and had not received proper federal recognition in 1934. Essentially, the argument was that the tribe were outsiders without a valid claim to be a legitimate tribe. Furthermore, it contended that the land acquired for them by the BIA in 1920 had never been the ancestral homeland of any Indians, had not been properly placed into trust, and had only recently been occupied by the tribe, rendering it ineligible as "Indian lands." The Supervisors informed their constituents that this litigation was their only recourse to stop the casino and protect the El Dorado County way of life.

By 2003, several similar cases in federal courts had ruled in favor of tribes. It became apparent that the Supervisors and their legal counsel recognized the possibility of their comprehensive legal assault on the tribe failing and the tribe's appeal in the Ninth Circuit prevailing. Nonetheless, they continued to employ strong rhetoric. In an April 2003 statement, the Supervisors aligned themselves firmly with constituents opposing "the disaster" of a casino. They enumerated various reasons for the intense local opposition, including concerns about gambling, increased crime, placing a large commercial development in a rural residential area, unfair competition with a tax-exempt tribe, further strain on already depleted public resources, and the visual and environmental impact of the massive casino complex, which was described as a "monstrosity."

In an attempt to undermine the tribe's sovereignty over its land, the Board asserted that they were outsiders without legitimate tribal status:

> "When this parcel of land was purchased by the federal government in 1920 for two unrelated groups of 34 individuals...who had no historic relationship to El Dorado County and no tribal relationship to one another, no one contemplated that 83 years later the consequences would be to allow anything like this."

Quoting the Lakes Entertainment financial analysis, the Supervisors highlighted that the casino was projected to generate $194 million in annual gross revenue. After operational costs, it would yield a net profit of $83.4 million, with thirty percent of this sum allocated to Lakes and Kean-Argovitz. The Board pointed out that this substantial annual profit for the casino investors would come at the expense of the El Dorado County environment.

Drawing from SUFC materials, the Board underscored the potential costs to County taxpayers, such as the casino's failure to provide employee health benefits, allow unionization, or contribute to addressing gambling addiction. They also emphasized the anticipated expenses for law enforcement to manage increased incidents of DUI, crime, and drug-related issues. Furthermore, the statement highlighted the competitive threat posed to local businesses by the casino, as it would offer restaurants and services without being subject to taxation. The Board reminded that the tribe had refused to waive its sovereign immunity, making it difficult to enforce any statements or promises made by the tribe.

Despite the confrontational tone, the Board's statement hinted at the possibility of finding common ground with the tribe. There were two clear indications of a potential compromise in its language. The first pertained to development fees:

> "The Board of Supervisors has struggled for years to ensure that the car carrying capacity of Highway 50, which the taxpayers of the State and County paid to build over the years, is not degraded by new development unless that new development pays the cost of replacing the capacity it uses up. The County therefore makes all new development pay for the road capacity it consumes by imposing road impact fees on new residential and commercial development."

The second hint at a potential compromise revolved around 'fair share agreements,' which had been successfully negotiated in neighboring counties with the Rumsey Band and the Enterprise Rancheria:

> "Tribal agreements were entered into in Yolo and Yuba Counties. Calculations show that if the Shingle Springs Band were to pay at the same rate per square foot as the Rumsey Band agreed to pay Yolo County, then they would pay El Dorado County an initial payment of $7 million plus $7.2 million annually. If the Shingle Springs Band were to pay at the same rate per square foot as the Enterprise Rancheria agreed to pay Yuba County, then they would pay El Dorado County an initial payment of $1.75 million plus $12.5 million annually."

The County was evidently suggesting the potential framework for a future agreement with the tribe.

What's 'Fair Share'?

El Dorado County was keenly observant of the deal struck between the Rumsey Band and Yolo County, and they closely monitored the ongoing compact negotiations between Governor Schwarzenegger and various California tribes.

Arnold Schwarzenegger, known for his background in bodybuilding and acting, and a leading member of the Republican Party, took office on October 7, 2003, following a special recall election to replace Democrat Governor Gray Davis. Schwarzenegger presented himself as fiscally conservative while adopting socially and culturally liberal stances. During his campaign, he pledged to address the state's financial challenges and frequently mentioned the prospect of a "fairer deal" between California and tribal gaming entities. Upon assuming office, he committed to renegotiating California's tribal gaming compacts with the aim of ensuring that tribes paid their "fair share."

Starting in early 2004, a team of attorneys led by Daniel Kolkey, a former federal appellate judge, engaged in negotiations with tribal attorneys to establish new compacts. Several of these negotiation sessions took place in the Sacramento law offices of Howard Dickstein, who served as the attorney for the Rumsey, Auburn, and Pala tribes.

Right from the outset, the tribes represented by Dickstein displayed a greater willingness to engage in renegotiation. This was partially attributed to Dickstein's prior success in securing a model revenue-sharing agreement with the Rumsey Tribe. On June 21, five gaming tribes — the Rumsey, United Auburn, Pala, Viejas, and Pauma bands — signed new compacts.

These new agreements included provisions for a $1 billion bond, backed by the five tribes, to aid the state's current budget. They also allowed for an increase in the number of video slots permitted in each casino and mandated annual payments of $275 million from the expected rise in profits. Although Schwarzenegger initially sought a 25% share, the $275 million amounted to approximately 15% of the tribes' net profits.

These compacts not only raised the portion of revenues allocated to state and local governments but also required tribes to hold labor union elections and resolve disputes with local governments through binding arbitration. Furthermore, the compacts affirmed the tribes' exclusive right to offer gaming services until 2030.

The remaining 56 tribes held back, with many vehemently opposing any renegotiation of the economic provisions within the compacts or any other alterations. George Forman, a prominent attorney specializing in Indian law who represented the Southern California tribes of Morongo and Sycuan, accused the Governor of pursuing a "divide and conquer" strategy that undermined government-to-government agreements based on the sovereignty of Indian nations on their respective lands.

The Rincon Band of Mission Indians, who owned Harrah's in San Diego County, reacted with fury to the new compacts and filed a lawsuit seeking to invalidate them, along with an immediate federal restraining order. Their argument centered on the Governor allegedly granting an unfair competitive advantage to the five tribes that signed the compacts over all the others that had agreed to the 1999 compacts. The Rincon Tribe, along with similar-minded tribes, were very open about their resentment at the prominent role played by Dickstein in the negotiations, whom they accused of secretly aligning with Cheryl Schmit.

Another group of tribes offered Schwarzenegger an additional $1 billion in cash (not in the form of bonds). They were willing to contribute no more than 10% of their profits in return. Their proposal also came with conditions, including a request for the state to adopt "less invasive" approaches to environmental concerns and to exclude the labor union provisions. This coalition consisted of Forman's clients, the Pechanga Band of Luiseno Indians of Temecula, and the Agua Caliente Band of Cahuilla Indians of Palm Springs. Simultaneously, sensing that Schwarzenegger might not accept their proposal, the Agua Caliente tribe was working to qualify a ballot measure that would lift slot machine limits. This measure would limit annual payments to around nine percent of California's corporate tax rate and impose no new labor and environmental regulations.

Additionally, eleven card clubs and five racetracks were circulating a proposition to break the tribes' monopoly on casino-style gaming unless they paid 25 percent of their profits to the state. In the event that tribes failed to meet this standard, card clubs and racetracks would gain the right to operate slot machines. Furthermore, one-third of their profits would be allocated for use by local public safety agencies, a provision aimed at winning public support.

Many tribal leaders accused the Governor of employing a "Divide and Conquer" strategy. Deron Marquez, Chairman of the San Manuel Band of Mission Indians, alleged that the state was creating tiers among tribes, differentiating between those allowed to expand, those permitted minimal expansion, and those seeking new compacts. The Governor's "fair share" message had resonated with the public, leading many tribes to believe it was time to halt the Governor's strategy.

A statewide commercial produced by San Manuel featured former Minnesota Governor Jesse Ventura opposing Schwarzenegger and his "fair share" message. Subsequently, the Governor ceased using the term when discussing tribes, and it was not publicly discussed again.

The contentious negotiations and their tumultuous aftermath were widely covered in El Dorado County. The County Supervisors closely monitored the agreements reached with local tribes, especially those represented by Dickstein, as they prepared for negotiations with the Shingle Springs Band concerning the interchange and the proposed casino.

A Deal

In late 2005 and much of 2006, both the County and the tribe engaged in negotiations to reach an agreement. The tribe had several primary objectives during these negotiations:

1. **Litigation Resolution:** The tribe aimed to resolve ongoing litigation related to the Highway 50 interchange, which was hindering progress.

2. **Legal Safeguards:** They sought assurances from the County that it wouldn't pursue further legal challenges against the planned casino.

3. **Sovereignty Recognition:** The tribe wanted formal recognition from the County as a federally recognized sovereign tribe. This recognition would pave the way for government-to-government relations between the tribe and the County.

On the other hand, the County had its own set of demands:

1. **Funding Commitment:** The County required the tribe to fully fund the Highway 50 interchange and cover these costs upfront before the casino's opening.

2. **Highway Expansion:** They also wanted the tribe to finance the construction of additional lanes on Highway 50 for High Occupancy Vehicles (HOVs).

3. **Other Payments:** The County insisted on various other financial commitments from the tribe.

4. **Ordinance Application:** They sought the tribe's agreement to adhere to specific County ordinances for the construction of the casino and other tribal projects.

To satisfy the County's constituents and gain their approval, the deal had to include substantial financial contributions from the tribe.

Both parties had reasons to move forward with the deal but also reasons to consider walking away. The County recognized that the tribe's ongoing federal lawsuit was likely to succeed, but they also feared that Lakes, the investor in the project, might pull out if further delays occurred. On the tribe's side, they hoped for a favorable ruling from the Ninth Circuit but were aware that the County could introduce legal and administrative hurdles. They also saw the potential for significant revenue sharing with the County, which could be beneficial when negotiating a future compact with the State. Moreover, they understood that further delays could jeopardize their relationship with their investor.

Ultimately, on September 28, 2006, the two parties reached an agreement and signed a Memorandum of Understanding, which stated:

> This Agreement represents the Parties' concerted effort to achieve a positive and constructive resolution of significant issues that have otherwise obstructed their government-to-government relationship to their collective and respective detriment. This Agreement will enhance that government-to-government relationship and effectuate a desire to maintain a continuing relationship that is both positive and responsive to the Parties' respective needs and desires.

The financial provisions outlined in the MOU included the following key points:

1. **HOV Lane Construction:** The tribe committed to funding the construction of 5.3 miles of High Occupancy Vehicle (HOV) lanes on both the eastbound and westbound sides of Highway 50. This funding would occur annually for 20 years, with the tribe providing $5.2 million each year for this purpose.

2. **Public Safety Compensation:** An annual payment of $600,000 would be made by the tribe to compensate for public safety law enforcement services.

3. **Support for Fire Protection and Emergency Medical Services:** The tribe agreed to engage in negotiations with other local entities to provide financial support for fire protection and emergency medical services.

4. **Sales and Hotel Tax:** In response to concerns from local businesses regarding unfair competition with tribal businesses, the tribe committed to collecting a sales and hotel tax. From the revenue generated by this tax, the tribe would contribute an additional $500,000 annually to the County.

Additional Funding: The tribe also agreed to provide additional funds to the County for the County's discretion, with the purpose of addressing the Tribe's Projects fully.

The financial terms of the agreement stipulated the following payment schedule:

- During the initial seven years of the casino's operation, the tribe would pay the County an annual sum of $2.2 million.
- From the eighth year through the twentieth year of the casino's operation, the annual payment would be reduced to $1.3 million.
- Commencing from the last day of the eighth year of the Gaming Project's operation and continuing for the duration of the tribe's Compact with the State or for a minimum of 20 years (whichever is longer), an additional annual payment of $2.5 million would be made. This payment would be subject to a 2% annual escalator, beginning with the ninth year.

It was a steep bill, amounting all told to around $250 million, but in exchange for these payments the County:

> "Hereby agrees to cease any and all efforts to oppose, delay or derail the tribe's Gaming and Interchange Projects in any forum or before any agency or governmental body whatsoever, whether federal, state, regional or municipal. The County also hereby agrees to refrain from assisting, encouraging, or aiding any other party from the foregoing. The County further specifically agrees it will ... seek dismissal of its pending appeal in the

> Ninth Circuit Court of Appeal....The County stipulates to the legitimacy of the tribe as a federally recognized Indian tribe entitled to game under IGRA and further stipulates to the legitimacy of the tribe's Rancheria as "Indian lands" upon which it may game under that same federal statutory authority."

Not all the local opponents of the tribe were satisfied with the agreement. Furthermore, some individuals with hostile intentions, recognizing the substantial financial commitments, started contemplating ways to benefit from the tribe's anticipated wealth.

Problems from the Past

As plans for the casino progressed, the tribe faced two historical problems. The first problem stemmed from the tribe's agreements with its initial investor in 1996-1997. The second issue raised questions about the tribe's distant origins.

In the final stages of negotiating with the County, the tribe encountered a mounting problem linked to its earlier Chrystal Mountain casino venture. Chris Anderson, who had financially supported the temporary casino in 1996, insisted on the return of his initial investment of $7 million. The tribe argued that the complete failure of the enterprise had nullified any repayment obligations and had canceled all agreements with Sharp Image in 1999.

Despite the lack of access roads, which not only led to the demise of the temporary casino but also hindered any other economic development on the rancheria, Anderson persisted in demanding his funds. As a result, the dispute continued, characterized by increasing harassment from Anderson and escalating demands for interest on his $7 million.

The news of the growing collaboration between the tribe and the County, along with the prospect of Lakes Entertainment installing up to 2000 video slots in a new, cutting-edge casino, further infuriated Anderson. His company, Sharp Image, initiated a lawsuit in El Dorado

County Superior Court. In this suit, he sought the return of his original investment with interest and the enforcement of his contract to supply casino slots to the casino. Anderson claimed damages amounting to $250 million.

The tribe and its legal representatives were mindful of the potential rights that California contract law might provide to Sharp Image. They also held concerns that local jurors in El Dorado County, who had experienced the ongoing disputes between the County and the tribe, might not be entirely impartial. Even a fraction of the damages Anderson claimed could jeopardize the plans for the new casino.

Additionally, in 2006-2007, an issue from the tribe's distant past resurfaced to complicate their casino plans. This issue pertained to the ethnic origins of the Shingle Springs Band. Questions arose regarding whether they were "genuine Indians" with ancestral ties to El Dorado County or if they were, in fact, "Ethnic Hawaiians" who were not true Miwoks. The outlines of a genealogical case against the tribe had already been outlined in the County's lawsuits.

Opponents of the casino, including local government officials, anti-gambling activists, the Grassy Run HOA, and Stand Up For California! seized upon an idea first introduced by the County in 2003 and bolstered by rumors. This notion posited that the Band were "outsiders" who had distinct ethnic origins from other Miwoks and were descended from "foreign" tribes. The argument centered around the assertions of a group of Indians who referred to themselves as "The Historic Shingle Springs Miwok."

These "Historic Miwoks" claimed to have been marginalized and mistreated by the newcomers but managed to secure significant funding, likely from local landowners, to pursue their case. Consequently, they filed amicus briefs and initiated numerous legal and administrative appeals, all with the aim of obtaining a share of what they believed would be the substantial profits from the casino.

The "Historic Miwuks" asserted that their heritage had been usurped by outsiders from Hawaii, namely the Shingle Springs Band, whom they labeled as 'Casino Indians' or 'The Sacramento-Verona Band.' Their claim revolved around allegations that these newcomers not only appropriated their tribal name but also "usurped the Historic Shingle Springs Miwok Tribe's federal recognition, ancestral lands, and consequently, its cultural identity."

Issues surrounding Indian identity often delve into history, sometimes scrutinizing family histories that involve marriages outside the tribe or examining historical census records of enrolled tribal members. In this case, the argument hinged on events from the distant past, prior to California's statehood, when the aboriginal population fell under the rule of the Mexican provincial government of Alta California.

It is an undisputed historical fact that in 1839, the Swiss entrepreneur John Sutter brought his Hawaiian mistress, Manuki, and a group of ten Hawaiian laborers to Alta California. They traveled up the Sacramento River to the site where Sutter later built his fort. Over time, additional Hawaiian laborers, who arrived from Hawaii via San Francisco, settled in what are now El Dorado and Yolo Counties. By 1848, when gold was discovered, this Hawaiian community had become quite sizable. Unable to bring wives from Hawaii, many of them married Native American women.

In 1862, a newspaper reporter, who had lived in Hawaii, came across a small village near what is now Verona. There, he counted 24 Hawaiian men and several Indian women who, despite being born in California and not in Hawaii, were proficient in the Hawaiian language. Over the next half-century, local newspapers occasionally made references to this community near Verona. In 1911, a journalist for the San Francisco Sunday Call visited the "Hawaiian Village" near Verona and reported on its continuation of Hawaiian traditions.

In 1916, John Terrell, a field agent for the Bureau of Indian Affairs (BIA), was in California searching for landless and destitute Indians who could be candidates for the federal plan to establish them on rancherias. He documented several Miwok families living in the

Placerville area, designating them as the El Dorado Band. A little less than 50 miles away, near Verona, he encountered a group predominantly of "Hawaiian and Maidu" descent, and he named them the Sacramento-Verona Band of Homeless Indians. He recommended purchasing land for them. Since Sacramento land was costly, the government acquired 160 acres in El Dorado County, adjacent to the 80-acre parcel intended for the El Dorado Miwok Indians.

The Sacramento-Verona tribe did not relocate to the 160-acre parcel but also resisted BIA efforts to sell it. Subsequently, after receiving federal recognition in 1976 and adopting the name Shingle Springs Band of Miwok Indians, a few of their over 500 tribal members began moving onto the land, initially residing in trailers and later constructing homes.

While it's evident that Hawaiian immigrants lived near Verona, the argument about genealogy and Hawaiian ethnic identity became less convincing after 150 years. Over six or seven generations, the descendants of these Hawaiians had intermarried with Maidu and Miwuk people. More importantly, the Historic Miwuks had not secured federal recognition themselves, and by the time they raised the issue, the statute of limitations for contesting federal recognition had long expired.

Nevertheless, these factors did not deter the Historic Miwuks from campaigning and seeking favor with opponents of the casino project. They presented themselves publicly, appearing at hearings before the County supervisors and elsewhere, asserting that they were the true Indians and even filed documents with the County claiming ownership of the tribe's land. They portrayed themselves as the Indians who had received federal recognition in 1934 under the Indian Reorganization Act (IRA) process.

In 2008, the tribe took legal action against one of the groups, led by Cesar Caballero, who claimed the title of 'chief,' and sought to prevent him from using the tribe's name. Despite a court ruling against Caballero, he persisted in his efforts. He managed to change the tribal mailing address to his own, obtained tax identification numbers from the Internal Revenue Service under the tribe's name, and created websites in the tribe's name. Caballero also submitted amici briefs in federal cases involving the Band's interests.

As the casino opened, the Shingle Springs Band filed a lawsuit in the United States District Court for the Eastern District. This lawsuit sought injunctive relief and monetary damages for the violation of the tribe's legal rights. The complaint targeted "individuals who had no connection with the tribe or permission to act on its behalf," and the court was asked to prohibit them from falsely representing or acting on behalf of the "Shingle Springs Band of Miwok Indians."

Caballero, who had initially refused to comply with the court's orders, was held in contempt and incarcerated. During the contempt proceedings, members of his group signed letters claiming to be the true "Shingle Springs Band of Miwok Indians." These individuals were again sued by the tribe in 2009. Ultimately, after further costly legal battles, the tribe prevailed in all its lawsuits against these impostors and those who attempted to obstruct or halt the tribe's casino operations.

The Shingle Springs Band, while acknowledging their traditional ties to Hawaii, legally defeated the 'Historic Miwuks' and dismantled the genealogical argument. They achieved this by adhering to federal regulations, establishing themselves as a tribe in accordance with proper procedures, employing an effective public relations strategy, and mounting a robust legal defense. This victory underscored the determination and persistence of tribal leadership, particularly Tribal Chairman Fonseca and the Tribal Council.

Even in the wake of victories, there may be ongoing challenges. In May 2020, more than a decade after the casino's opening, a reporter from a Hawaiian news source and podcast visited El Dorado County to explore 'the Hawaiian diaspora.' During an interview with Marilyn Ferguson, a docent at a historical museum in Placerville, she asserted, "They were known as the lost tribe of kanakas. They're not our Indians. They're not local." Controversial opinions can persist long after disputes have been settled.

Defending Tribal Sovereignty: Battling Sharp Image and Legal Challenges

The grand opening of Red Hawk Casino in January 2009 marked another triumph of the tribe's resilience and perseverance. This success did not bring an end to their challenges.

The casino's performance fell significantly short of Lakes Entertainment's earnings projections, and reports surfaced that Lakes had to lend money to the tribe when the casino failed to meet its monthly revenue minimums. Amidst these difficulties, the legal dispute with their initial investor, Sharp Image, reached a critical juncture.

Recognizing that the El Dorado Superior Court was not an ideal venue, and that California contract law might favor Sharp Image, the tribe sought recourse with federal authorities and federal courts.

The tribe contended that the agreements with Anderson had been illegal from the beginning, as they had never received approval from the NIGC under federal law. In April 2009, the NIGC determined that the contracts with Sharp Image had indeed violated federal law and were therefore void and unenforceable.

The tribe and its legal team believed that the NIGC's determination should have been sufficient to win their case when introduced in court. Superior Court Judge Morrison C. England ruled that the NIGC's finding was improper and could not be considered in the proceedings. On August 7, 2010, after a jury found that the tribe had wrongly terminated its contract with the gaming machine supplier, they were ordered to pay $30.4 million to Sharp Image Gaming (plus interest over the entire period, totaling more than $40 million). In response, the tribe appealed to federal court, noting that the company had been deemed an unsuitable vendor by California's Bureau of Gambling Control.

All the tribe's worst fears about the local state courts were realized, and they now faced the looming threat of Judge England executing the judgment. The tribe's legal representatives filed documents with the Superior Court, outlining a "doomsday scenario" in which the casino's cash and assets could be seized, potentially leading to the facility's closure. The lawyers argued that "any attempts to execute the judgment at this time would likely result in catastrophic consequences for the tribe and all those who rely on the casino for their livelihoods."

It would take an additional six years before the tribe finally emerged victorious in this protracted legal battle. Even to this day, Anderson continues to threaten further litigation.

Diversifying Economic Ventures: Expanding Beyond the Casino

The casino's failure to meet its financial expectations prompted the tribe to explore additional economic opportunities on its reservation. In 2015, the tribe acquired 25 acres of land, situated just one off-ramp to the west of its casino. Subsequently, in 2016, when the federal government took the land into trust, rumors began to circulate about potential developments on this site, including a hotel, restaurants, and other commercial ventures. Predictably, opposition to these plans started to stir.

In reality, the tribe initially planned its primary development on this land to be a gas station and a convenience store. This project made economic sense, as it had a built-in customer base among the casino's 1,200 employees.

By mid-2016, the facility located at Shingle Springs Drive and Highway 50 was constructed and ready to serve customers. Local opposition delayed its opening. Concerned residents, aiming to preserve the area's character, mobilized against the project. A rural preservation group, El Dorado Council Inc., filed a lawsuit against El Dorado County to halt the opening. The lawsuit argued that the County had failed to mandate a comprehensive environmental review under the California Environmental Quality Act (CEQA) before granting permits.

It took a full year of negotiations with local residents before the Express Fuel Station and convenience store could finally open in June 2017. The tribe's negotiating strategy centered on the fact that local homes relied on well water and lacked sewage lines. The high cost of drilling wells into an uncertain aquifer, coupled with the frequent need for septic tank maintenance and soil percolation challenges, made the tribe's settlement offer appealing to residents. Under the agreement, residents were granted access to water and sewage pipes for the gas station on the condition that the tribe could proceed with opening the Fuel Express facility. This arrangement added very little to the project's $7 million cost since residents had to cover the expenses of connecting their homes to the new utilities. It helped secure support and approval while fostering positive community relations.

Other aspects of the settlement included the tribe's commitment to sell local El Dorado County products in its new mini-mart, giving hiring preference to El Dorado County residents, and funding gates for several nearby neighborhoods to help restrict casino traffic to the reservation. Following the gas station and mini-mart, the tribe successfully opened a dog park and car wash without any controversy.

For years, health-care services in the Shingle Springs area were limited to a small clinic located off the reservation. In response to the growing demand for healthcare, the tribe established and operated the Shingle Springs Health and Wellness Clinic on Honpie Road at the southern edge of the Rancheria.

Between 2015 and 2017, the tribe began purchasing parcels of neighboring undeveloped real estate to regain reservation land that had been taken from them in the past. Ideally, these purchases would have occurred well before the casino's development, as it's a well-known real estate phenomenon that land values rise significantly near casinos. For instance, ten acres of land east of Shingle Springs Drive and north of Red Hawk Casino had an assessed value of $113,000, but the tribe paid $1.5 million for it. The tribe did not deny that at some point in the future, it might plan commercial developments on some of this land. It emphasized that its primary purpose was to construct housing for tribal members, a majority of whom reside away from the rancheria. This emphasis on residential development appeared to temper land prices. In early 2018, the tribe purchased 35.9 acres north of the casino for $1.2 million.

Realizing Dreams: Achieving Economic Stability and Community Prosperity

As of 2020, the tribe had achieved economic stability. They had signed a new compact with Governor Newsom, effectively resolving many of the issues with local residents. Furthermore, they had initiated numerous quality-of-life programs benefiting both tribal members and the local communities. This marked the culmination of years of dedicated effort, opening new opportunities.

Chairwoman Regina Cuellar expressed gratitude to Governor Newsom for endorsing the new compact. She highlighted the extensive range of transformative services and programs available to tribal members, including those related to education, youth development, higher education, family health and wellness, an initiative for 'Honored Elders,' environmentally sustainable practices, tribal police and fire departments, and the preservation and promotion of their history, culture, and traditions. Cuellar emphasized that this compact would enable them to continue supporting an integrated program involving financial contributions, volunteerism, and community engagement in non-profit and other community sectors. Notable among these efforts were the Shingle Springs Health & Wellness Center, which provided medical, dental, behavioral health, and pharmacy services to thousands in the area, as well as the tribe's Temporary Assistance to Needy Families (TANF) programs, extending their reach beyond El Dorado County to Placer, Sacramento, and Yolo counties.

Signifying that they had largely overcome their economic challenges, the tribe announced Phase II of their development plans. These plans encompassed the construction of a five-story, 45,000-square-foot hotel with 156 rooms and a conference center. Additionally, they included an upscale restaurant, retail and office spaces, and an entertainment venue within a 46,200-square-foot building, as well as two fast-food restaurants, one spanning 3,230 square feet and the other 3,275 square feet. Atop the garage, they expanded to create the APEX, featuring 18 bowling lanes, a race track for car enthusiasts, three virtual reality chairs, and a spacious sports bar equipped with multiple large-screen televisions for enjoying your favorite games.

After years of perseverance, the tribe was starting to enjoy economic security, and its members were experiencing increasing prosperity. At long last, the tribe was on the path to self-reliance.

CHAPTER SIX

Strategies for Success: Lessons and Insights

The ultimate victory of these three tribes can be attributed to their unique relationship with the federal government, a historical relationship enshrined in the U.S. Constitution. This special relationship granted tribes certain rights and protections that local communities or entities, no matter how hard they would try, could not simply undermine or strip away.

Under this constitutionally protected relationship, Native American tribes are recognized as distinct political entities with a degree of self-governance and autonomy. This means that they have the authority to make decisions and enact laws within their territories, known as reservations, without interference from state or local governments. While this sovereignty is not absolute and is subject to federal oversight, it provides tribes with a powerful legal and political tool to protect their interests and pursue their goals.

For these tribes, tribal sovereignty allowed them to assert their rights to land, self-determination, and economic development, including the operation of casinos. Local communities and opponents might have attempted to impede their progress, but the legal framework of tribal sovereignty acted as a shield, safeguarding their efforts and preserving their rights.

In essence, the victory of these tribes underscores the importance of tribal sovereignty as a cornerstone of Native American rights and self-determination. It's a testament to the enduring strength of this constitutional relationship that empowers tribes to shape their own destinies and protect their cultural and economic interests.

Within the narratives of these three tribes, there exist diverse paths to achieving self-reliance. This chapter aims to distill valuable lessons from their experiences, focusing on the strategies and approaches that proved effective for each of them.

These lessons offer practical insights for various stakeholders, including tribal governments embarking on casino ventures or seeking to expand existing operations, acquire additional land, and diversify their economies. They are also relevant for tribes confronting political, legal, or regulatory challenges. Elected or appointed leaders outside tribal boundaries who collaborate with tribal governments will find valuable takeaways. Furthermore, this knowledge can benefit all those engaged in 'Indian Country' – encompassing business professionals, consultants, legal experts, journalists, and academics.

Equally important, the histories of these tribes hold lessons for younger generations. None of us want to hear how our parents had to walk 5 miles each way to go to school. But we should all appreciate how much easier we have it because of their sacrifices. Understanding the trials and tribulations their parents and grandparents endured to bring their tribe to its present state is crucial. The arduous struggles and persistent threats to tribal sovereignty, often concealed from younger generations, deserve recognition and comprehension.

Tribal gaming marked the beginning of their journey toward self-reliance. However, tribes recognize that they must continuously position themselves to make sound decisions for the well-being of future generations. Tribal gaming has enabled these communities to return to their reservations (with Jamul still in progress), providing essential resources, establishing stable governments, and ensuring access to education and healthcare for their members.

San Manuel

The case history of the San Manuel tribe traces its remarkable journey from owning a small apricot orchard in the San Bernardino foothills to becoming one of California's foremost gaming tribes. Today, they have significant influence on both regional and state economies, with their impact extending into the neighboring State of Nevada, as well as on the federal level.

The San Manuel tribe's remarkable ascent can be divided into two distinct periods:

1995-2000: Pioneering Legalization

The tribe's journey began with audacious decisions made by its tribal leadership. They ventured into bingo operations, securing borrowed funds and recruiting expertise from the Seminoles, showcasing their fearlessness. Defying Governor Wilson and confronting federal marshals to safeguard their slot machines was viewed by many as both daring and perhaps even foolhardy. Recognizing the need for innovation, they invested substantially in a comprehensive TV and radio educational campaign to gain the trust of California's citizens. This move not only underscored their innovative spirit but also demonstrated their unwavering commitment to forging a new path and setting a precedent for Native American tribes.

Arguably, their boldest step was to candidly discuss some of the harsh realities of their history with the people of California. The tribal leaders understood, better than most consultants and attorneys, that a history lesson highlighting past injustices could justify their plea for fairness in the present, opening doors to self-reliance.

San Manuel's electoral campaigns were shrewdly framed around the undeniable facts of history to garner public support for tribal gaming. They argued that Native Americans, who had suffered enslavement and exploitation by the Spanish and dispossession and displacement by Anglo-Americans, deserved an opportunity for self-reliance. Research indicated that the term "self-reliance" resonated powerfully with Californians. The public education campaign employed words such as 'fairness,' 'self-help,' and 'economic independence.' In these terms, San Manuel spearheaded efforts that twice convinced over three-fifths of California's electorate to endorse tribal gaming. Notably, the idea of seeking 'reparations' was never raised.

The key takeaway here is that Native American tribes should not shy away from recounting the truth about their tragic history. The tribe's early successes were not guaranteed. Without the financial backing generated from their bold and risky decisions, without their defiance of state and federal authorities, statewide campaigns would not have materialized. Money alone would have been insufficient without San Manuel's leadership. They managed to forge a formidable tribal coalition in support of Propositions 5 and 1A. Following San Manuel's lead and insights, the Pechanga tribe made financial commitments and joined forces followed by the Morongo tribe, collectively reducing the burden of risk. This robust coalition, traversing the state, garnered the backing of CNIGA and the majority of California tribes. Tribes from across the nation watched in awe at the unfolding events in California.

The episode underscores the importance of tribal connections. The Serrano people, divided into the Maarrênga'yam ("people from Morongo") and the Yuhaaviatam ("people of the pines" or the San Manuel), were the largest contributors to the 1998-2000 campaigns. For Proposition 5, San Manuel spent $27,783,000, and Morongo contributed $12,621,000, together accounting for two-thirds of the total campaign expenditures. For Proposition 1A, San Manuel spent $8,711,000, and Morongo contributed $4,620,000, collectively comprising more than half of all expenditures. It was the exemplary unity of the two Serrano tribes that kept the coalition intact through two grueling campaigns, aided by the Pechanga tribe, followed by the vast majority of tribes in the state.

The key lesson here is that tribes possess more significant political influence when they collaborate. Tribal alliances amplify the political impact they can collectively achieve. Associations hold immense political and financial power.

Campaigns were not the sole avenue to legalize gaming. San Manuel's well-orchestrated educational and lobbying efforts joined by other tribes involved in compact discussions successfully shepherded the compacts through negotiation and ratification, securing legislative approval for Proposition 1A. Effective tribal lobbying hinges on educating legislators and officials about tribal sovereignty, tribal governance, federal law's application to states, and the unique rights and needs of tribes and their members.

1995-2000: Effective Tribal Advocacy and Education

My company prepared tribal leaders to tell their stories and organized dozens of trips to Sacramento and Washington D.C. to educate elected officials and present the tribal case. This educational initiative was instrumental in breaking down barriers to Indian gaming in California. The leadership of each tribe recognized the importance of cultivating relationships with state legislators and agency officials.

In simple terms, the lesson learned is that effective tribes excel in advocating for themselves. They educate others about their rights and demonstrate unwavering commitment to enhancing their communities and achieving self-reliance. Despite their apprehension about speaking in public, they summon the courage to step forward, extend their hand, and share their story. As I often remind them, with each story, it becomes easier. I am not sure they believe me, but it is true.

Evolution of Tribal Political Contributions

Between 1998 and 2000, the involvement of tribal funds in politics was met with significant criticism, viewed by opponents as a testament to the corrupting influence of gambling. Accusations arose that tribes had essentially "bought" political support. This scrutiny extended to Gray Davis, who faced allegations that his robust support for state-tribal compacts was driven by tribal contributions during his 1998 campaign. His even larger tribal donations during his 2002 campaign contributed to his recall in 2003, with some of his supporters referring to it as "the curse of Indian money." Notably, while tribal contributions were closely examined, substantial donations from entities like PG&E, Edison, SEIU, California Teachers Association, and the California Federation of Labor went largely unquestioned.

Over time, concerns surrounding 'Indian money' in politics appear to have waned. Larger sums of Indian contributions have attracted less controversy, with tribes and gaming companies frequently ranking among the nation's top campaign contributors. For example, in 2008, gaming tribes were the largest contributors in California politics, and two individual California tribes, Morongo and Pechanga, were among the four largest contributors nationwide. This diminishing scrutiny aligns with the broader political landscape, where very substantial campaign financing, such as that of Presidents Obama and Biden, has faced minimal criticism.

As the volume of Indian money in both California and national politics has grown, San Manuel maintains its involvement in state and federal government affairs, albeit with relatively smaller political contributions. Continued education of elected officials and their staff remains crucial for building lasting relationships, particularly in term-limited legislatures where turnover is frequent. The key takeaway is that successful tribes, through ongoing education, can afford to allocate fewer funds to electoral politics, instead directing resources toward their members and charitable causes.

Inter-Tribal Conflict and Public Relations

While San Manuel played a pivotal role in uniting the majority of tribes in a coalition during the earlier period, divisions among tribes have since become more pronounced. Notably, inter-tribal conflict can lead to poor public relations, especially when disputes spill into the open and involve financial battles. An illustrative example of such discord occurred when four tribes (Pechanga, Morongo, Sycuan, and Agua

Caliente) supported Propositions 94, 95, 96, contributing a combined $108 million. These propositions allowed each tribe to operate additional slot machines and were opposed by two other tribes (Pala and Auburn) who collectively spent $13 million against them. The media coverage scrutinized both sides, focusing on the perceived corrupting influence of tribal money. The result was that all propositions failed.

The lesson here is clear: tribal disunity, particularly when it escalates into public financial conflicts, can severely damage public relations and become a significant political liability for tribal gaming.

In the late 1990s, San Manuel played a substantial role in funding lobbying efforts in Sacramento. In recent years, other tribes and tribal coalitions have become the primary contributors to legislative and agency lobbying efforts. Notably, during conflicts such as the battle with California's card clubs and the effort to preserve tribal gaming exclusivity, other tribes have taken the lead in applying lobbying pressure on state agencies and key legislators. These instances highlight the evolution of lobbying dynamics within tribal gaming.

In summary, these lessons underscore the importance of effective tribal advocacy, collaboration, and ongoing education. Successful tribes are adept at advocating for their rights, educating others about their history and sovereignty, and building relationships with elected officials. Additionally, tribal unity and effective public relations are vital for maintaining a positive image in the eyes of the public and policymakers. Finally, tribes must adapt to changing lobbying landscapes while preserving their interests and exclusivity in the gaming industry.

San Manuel, once the tribe that outspent all other California tribes during the early period, has evolved significantly. They initially led the way in political achievements, utilizing their resources effectively, and today, they channel their gaming revenues into social and educational programs, bolstering their positive public reputation, an asset for future endeavors.

A further sign of the coming of age of San Manuel, is its entry into state politics via the election of a tribal member. The tribe's former

Chairman, James Ramos, was recently elected to his second term in the California State Assembly. Prior to that he served as a San Bernardino County Supervisor and before that, he served on the local community college board. The leadership skills he acquired as Chairman of the San Manuel Band of Mission Indians served him well in his run for offices beyond the tribe and prepared him to deal with issues of significance to the larger community of which San Manuel is a part. He has taken the lead in authoring lots of important legislation to assist California's tribal governments including a bill to require California's public schools to teach the true history of the genocidal horrors perpetrated against Native Americans.

James Ramos stands as a beacon of inspiration within the tribal community. His unwavering courage and strength have galvanized many tribal leaders to venture beyond their reservations, engage in public office, serve on commissions, immerse in local politics, and enrich the broader community with invaluable lessons from their native lands. In the coming years, it's likely we'll see more Native Americans, inspired by leaders like James Ramos, stepping up to run for prominent national offices. The idea of a Native American in the White House might once have seemed distant, but with figures like Ramos paving the way, it's a future we can envision. Could we one day chant "James Ramos for President"? You never know.

The development and elaboration of its governing structures may be one of San Manuel's most striking achievements. Today, it has the most sophisticated machinery of self-government of any California tribe. A very experienced elected leadership works closely with a highly professional staff to oversee the Gaming Commission and the Fire Department as well as a Department of Health, a Department of Public Safety, and a Department of Project/Construction and Development.

San Manuel has given especially careful thought to the development of its judiciary. The Tribal Court exercises general civil jurisdiction over its own citizens and "anyone who has consented to tribal jurisdiction:" this includes those who have entered the San Manuel Reservation or anyone engaging in contractual relations with the Tribe (excepting gaming-related disputes, which are handled and heard by the Gaming Commission). The judicial arm consists of a Trial Court and Appellate Court: the latter hears appeals from final judgments and final orders of the Trial Court; and the Chief Judge of the Trial Court acts as the Chief Administrator of both courts.

San Manuel's governance, especially its development of a judiciary that is winning approbation for independence and protecting tribal sovereignty, is a striking example of the tribe's coming of age institutionally. It has served to build the tribe's reputation for competence and integrity.

Also striking is the consistency and coherence of the ideas underpinning San Manuel's educational and philanthropic policies. Tribal leaders express 'world views' that have only strengthened over the years. The tribe has continued to champion the teaching of local Native American history, which it first began in the 1998 campaign. It continues to insist on the vital importance of sovereignty, also first emphasized in campaign ads. In its interactions with local and regional governments, it regularly reminds them of its governmental independence while also proving its capacity as a self-governing entity. Its commitments to the health and safety of its own membership are paralleled by substantial efforts to help non-Indians in neighboring areas. The education of young tribal members to lead the next generation remains a well-funded priority.

San Manuel has managed its relations with neighboring communities with exceptional success. The 2017 land swap between San Manuel and San Bernardino was presented as being mutually beneficial. In fact, the tribe, although cash rich and land poor, was clearly growing in economic importance and the municipality was equally clearly in decline. Essentially, the tribe's revenue stream from gaming is now more reliable than the city's tax revenues, and the tribe is better able than the city to control its expenditures. In a further demonstration of the tribe's growing economic power, in March 2021 its council proposed the development of a warehouse of 1.1 million square feet on 53 acres jointly owned with the San Bernardino International Airport Authority and the Inland Valley Development Agency.

The San Manuel leadership knows that its first duty for the future is to sustain the strong, reliable flow of revenue from its gaming operations that permit it to expand its interests. It continues to nurture its gaming facilities as its basic engine of economic development while it also works to diversify its economy through other ventures.

Since opening its doors, San Manuel has maintained a highly professional casino operation, with efficient staff overseen by seasoned general managers, and is widely reputed to produce more revenues than its top-tier competitors. Yet, unlike all the other major gaming tribes in California, San Manuel decided against building an on-site hotel and resort complex. In part, the explanation for this is that they had limited land for development and the location of their reservation allowed them to depend on customers commuting from Los Angeles, San Bernardino, Riverside and Orange Counties.

It was only in November 2017 that the tribe announced plans to build a hotel. In 2019, the tribe held a ceremony to begin officially a major expansion to include the hotel and a "world class world-class entertainment venue, an array of state-of-the-art amenities, including new dining experiences, retail and event spaces." It seems very likely that San Manuel will now draw even greater revenues from its casino complex and that the tribe will continue well into the future to add to its economic and philanthropic programs. In testimony to the tribe's economic success, they announced in 2021 their purchase for $650 million of the Las Vegas Palms Resort. The Vegas gambling interests that opposed San Manuel now face competition on their own doorstep.

The tribe's continuing low-key involvement in Sacramento and its leadership in its regional community need to be seen as ways of maintaining a presence and sustaining support for Indian gaming.

The San Manuel leadership knows that it is not impossible that tribes could lose their monopoly because of legislative decision making; it is even imaginable that some future referendum could end Indian gaming entirely. The tribe maintains a realistic perspective on the ongoing and vital need for public support for tribal gaming while concurrently pursuing diversification into non-gaming sectors of the economy. San Manuel learned in the 1990s that the people of California could be persuaded to vote to support Indian gaming; equally, they understand that fifty percent plus one vote could end it.

The lesson learned underscores that building positive relations isn't a one-time endeavor; rather, it's an enduring responsibility. This involves consistently contributing to local communities, engaging in ongoing dialogues, and not only liaising with official authorities but equally crucial, maintaining a meaningful connection with the people of California. After all, these individuals are their neighbors, and their voting decisions are influenced by the tribe's actions and communication efforts.

In the past two decades, many tribes have sought to emulate San Manuel's successes. The case histories for Jamul Village and Shingle Springs show that, in several respects, the path to legalized Indian gaming is becoming more, not less arduous.

Jamul Indian Village of California

The Jamul tribe's journey raises several pertinent questions. Why did this tribe face such prolonged challenges in establishing its casino? What compelled them to accumulate a half billion dollars in debt in the process? And why, even today, do they find themselves entangled in legal battles initiated against them? These questions inevitably draw attention to the tribe's opponents and their underlying motives to obstruct the tribe and its casino.

In considering the opposition faced by Jamul, one must ponder the significance of racism as a motivating factor. To dismiss the notion that racially-based, anti-Indian sentiments were absent among elected and appointed officials within California's state and county governments would be overly simplistic. It is a reasonable assumption that some members of the local community held substantial biases rooted in racism.

In contrast to the first Governor of California, there was no explicit presence of racism in the statements made by state and local officials. Supervisor Jacob, for example, consistently emphasized her close relationships with all the other tribes in the county, expressed unwavering support for tribal casinos, and professed a strong concern for the welfare of Native Americans. Similarly, signs at citizen demonstrations in Jamul prominently proclaimed that the opposition was 'anti-casino, not anti-Indian.'

Nevertheless, despite the absence of overt racism, local politics strongly favored the tribe's opponents. It became evident that Jamul was contending with a system that aligned with the preferences and sentiments of the county's leadership, particularly their local Supervisor and the white middle and upper-middle-class newcomers. These newcomers either overlooked or intentionally disregarded the fact that the Kumeyaay had inhabited the valley for 12,000 years prior to their arrival. Many tribes today grapple with analogous challenges, and Jamul's journey provides valuable insights.

The term 'systemic racism' is frequently used without deep analysis. The central issue in the Jamul case history lies in the fact that local power structures were reluctant to acknowledge and treat Jamul as an equal government entity. This problem extended beyond tribal members not being part of the local property-owning class; it also stemmed from their absence on local boards or state agencies. A more profound issue was that local white majorities were accustomed to having their preferences respected by county and state officials. Conversely, those officials, primarily white themselves, were unaccustomed to interacting with the local Indian tribe that had remained largely ignored or invisible for decades. It's in this context that the system can be described as having elements of racism.

Local interests were accustomed to wielding significant influence over decisions related to zoning, building permits, and various environmental requirements. They and their locally elected representatives were taken aback when a small tribe, previously almost imperceptible to the white population, asserted their right to construct on their property as they saw fit.

In the case of an Indian tribe neither inflamed local majorities nor the adverse actions of entrenched local officials have the final say, as long as the tribe possesses the resources to persist against their opposition. Jamul's leaders recognized that their ultimate protection lay in their federal recognition, the federal constitution, Congressional statutes, and Supreme Court opinions.

From a political standpoint, it posed a significant challenge for the tribe that individuals like Jacob and other opponents could assert that they represented the overwhelming majority of local residents. In the United States, majority opinion often carries a sense of legitimacy, echoing Abraham Lincoln's assertion that "Real or imagined, public opinion influences every aspect of our society."

For the tribe's opponents, it was a source of frustration that despite their belief in having majority support within their community and an abundance of financial and legal resources, all the typical tools of politics repeatedly failed to deliver the decisive blow against the casino project in the face of the tribe's unwavering determination. This included supportive local media coverage, near-unanimous grassroots demonstrations, longstanding connections with influential figures in Sacramento and San Diego County, and support from local law enforcement — all of which proved ineffective in halting the project.

In the beginning, it's possible that only a few of the casino's opponents truly grasped the concept of tribal sovereignty or Jamul's status as a government accountable solely to Congress. In fact, it seems likely that some members of JAC never gained such an understanding or simply chose to disregard it, which is a more probable scenario. Their attorney may not have initially comprehended it and consistently refused to acknowledge it, even after filing numerous lawsuits that consistently failed to halt the tribe. Certain local officials may not have initially realized that, from a federal law perspective, the balance of power was tipped in favor of the tribe, a federally recognized sovereign nation with the backing of federal law.

Since the tribe had no economic resources of its own, it relied on financial support from developers and gaming operators to build their casino. These developers and investors, lacking a substantial background in Indian gaming operations, approached Jamul as they would a non-Indian gaming project.

The lesson drawn from the Jamul experience is clear: if more resources had been provided by the investors, a public education campaign regarding the facts of tribal history could have achieved better and faster results for Jamul. It would have been beneficial to inform local officials and activists about the tribe's constitutionally protected status and recognition as a tribal government.

It was not a lack of knowledge about federal law that sustained ongoing opposition to Jamul's plans. By 2006, local attorney Patrick Webb must have been aware that his lawsuits lacked any viable legal claims. His clients, too, must have realized the futility of their efforts after numerous failures before administrative agencies and in the courts. Nevertheless, long after they understood the weakness of their legal position, Jacob, Webb, and others continued to obstruct the tribe's plans, filing complaints and lawsuits, all of which were dismissed or defeated. They used these lawsuits to keep the opposition group united, using them as propaganda, with each suit touted as the one that would stop the casino. To this day, the group is still searching for that supposed silver bullet.

In fact, not only did opposition to the casino persist for another decade after 2006, but it intensified. This occurred because funds were made available for a calculated strategy aimed at increasing investor costs and causing delays. Webb's lawsuits (many of which were doomed from the start because they were filed in state courts), the hostile local public relations stunts, the lobbying efforts with the BIA and CalTrans — all were geared toward draining investors' resources and forcing them to abandon Jamul. It was a strategy with a realistic chance of success.

The total expenditures on this opposition strategy are difficult to ascertain since they are largely concealed within fees paid to lobbyists, attorneys, and consultants. They undoubtedly amounted to tens of millions of dollars. What must be emphasized here is that the strategy came perilously close to success. In fact, in 2012, the strategy succeeded in forcing Lakes, the tribe's investor, to exit.

Most observers of Jamul's protracted struggle have been perplexed by the massive funding of relentless opposition. Perhaps the most astute observers of the Jamul case are the judges of the Ninth Circuit Court of Appeals, a circuit that encompasses more gaming tribes than any other. They have expressed a sense of bewilderment tinged with exasperation. As recently as August 8, 2020, the Ninth Circuit was reviewing a JAC case alleging that Jamul was not a historic tribe. The justices dismissed the argument in an opinion they hoped would "finally put an end to these claims."

> "No tribunal has accepted this argument. But that has not deterred litigants, including JAC and other members of the plaintiff organizations, from pressing similar claims in myriad actions before administrative agencies, state courts, and federal courts around the country since the early 1990s."

It was announced at JAC meetings many local homeowners had financially supported the organization and Patrick Webb offered some of his legal help for free. There were rumors that implied other tribes in San Diego might have played a role in obstructing or delaying the Jamul tribe's project.

Ultimately, unlike corporate developers, Jamul's leaders understood that with persistence and the law on their side, they could assert a claim to legitimacy that superseded local authorities. The federal Constitution clearly outlines a federal-tribal relationship that safeguards tribes from hostile local communities. Congress alone possesses the authority to define the limits of tribal sovereignty, as established by the 'Commerce Clause' in Article I of the Constitution, which empowers Congress to "regulate commerce with ... the Indian tribes."

Jamul's case history imparts crucial lessons in tribal leadership. The tribe faced formidable government agencies and well-financed private interests, but its leaders demonstrated unwavering persistence, refusing to yield to endless obstruction and delays. They showcased entrepreneurial acumen, seizing every available opportunity to advance their plans, all while prioritizing the unity and support of their tribal members.

It's essential to acknowledge the sacrifices made by the entire tribe to build their casino. Due to its size and the BIA's refusal to take additional land into trust, the casino had to encompass the entire 6 acres of the reservation. Tribal members residing in HUD houses on the reservation willingly forfeited their housing and relocated off the reservation when construction of the casino began, in the hope of securing a better future for all tribal members and future generations. Every tribal member moved away from the reservation to different areas in San Diego County, and some even relocated out of state. They made this sacrifice with the belief that the casino would succeed, even though nearly two decades later, they are still unable to return home as the tribe awaits the process of placing additional land into trust.

Jamul's leadership was acutely aware that delivering a profitable casino was imperative, as they would be held accountable by the tribe. The key lesson here is the significance of uniting the tribal membership behind a tribal project.

With unwavering determination, the tribe demonstrated that the most effective approach was a legal strategy that shifted the battleground from state courts to the federal district court and eventually to the federal Court of Appeals. Jamul Indian Village, though it took time and considerable resources, found justice through the federal court system, which consistently upheld the provisions of IGRA. In the end, it was the justices of the Ninth Circuit who compelled local non-Indian power structures to adhere to federal law.

Shingle Springs Tribe

One fundamental question arising from this case history is why, despite encountering numerous obstacles and facing vehement hostility, the tribe never contemplated walking away. Today, their leaders emphasize that they drew inspiration from their elders and ancestors who instilled in them the value of resilience, the importance of protecting future generations. Their long memories held the unwavering truth about their history, including how a state agency had unjustly deprived them of access to their ancestral lands.

The Shingle Springs case serves as a stark reminder of the enduring consequences of historical injustices. In the mid-19th century, California's Indigenous peoples fell victim to profound federal deceit: tribal treaties with the United States were quickly forgotten after being made. In the early 20th century, after the allegedly 'lost' treaties resurfaced, feeble attempts were made to 'compensate' tribes with allotments of rancherias, often in remote wilderness areas.

By that time, the widespread land expropriation and forced dispersion of tribal communities had obliterated their original locations. The fact that these actions were a result of federal policies seemed to trouble the conscience of few federal bureaucrats who 'discovered' landless tribes or granted federal 'recognition' to them.

Specifically, the Shingle Springs case should serve as a potent reminder that the later 20th century did not absolve the injustices perpetrated against tribes in earlier times. It was during the mid-1960s, a period often hailed as a time of liberal policies, that Cal-Trans, with complete disregard for federal land allocations, confiscated a significant portion of the Shingle Springs tribe's designated rancheria and routed a highway through the land it seized. This state action, which went uncompensated and unquestioned by federal authorities, left tribal members without access to their land, laying the foundation for many of the challenges the tribe had to confront, ultimately necessitating the tribe to pay for access to its own reservation for the sake of its future success.

One potential lesson from this situation is that the Shingle Springs tribe may not have effectively conveyed their story in a manner that could have shifted public perceptions or garnered support from the civil rights community.

The bureaucrats at CalTrans exhibited an astonishing level of resistance to organized pressures. Even as late as the 1990s, CalTrans refused to acknowledge the tribe or recognize their status as a government, consistently declining meetings with tribal leaders. Even in the early 2000s, during Governor Davis's tenure, despite significant campaign contributions from California tribes, he vetoed legislation aimed at compelling CalTrans to recognize tribes as governments and engage in dialogue with tribal leaders.

Initially, and to some extent, state officials might have been acting out of ignorance regarding the tribe's federally protected status. This cannot explain the prolonged stubbornness of state officials or Davis's veto. A more plausible explanation is that El Dorado County officials and affluent property owners in the Grassy Run area held more sway with the state than the poor Indians in Shingle Springs. It's also likely that established tribes in the broader Sacramento region exerted considerable adverse influence (possibly delaying the opening of the Wilton tribe's casino, also in the Sacramento area, from 2010 to 2021).

Shingle Springs encountered underhanded tactics in their initial efforts to bring homes onto the reservation and open a casino. Grassy Run was an upscale neighborhood with high-end residences and a private road set in a tranquil environment. Some initial opposition could be understood, as residents never envisioned their road being shared with others, let alone becoming a thoroughfare to a casino or other economic development in the area. Property owners in many other areas have faced similar challenges from non-Indian developers without resorting to malicious tactics or violence that warranted FBI investigations.

We can only speculate about the motivations of those who threw rocks at tribal members' cars and at the customers of the first casino. When approaching the Big Tent on its opening day, I observed middle-class white individuals who would never have considered targeting white-owned businesses with such actions. Their behavior indicated a belief that they would face no arrests by the County Sheriff's officers or the FBI and that they could act against the tribe and its visitors without consequence. Such attitudes are associated with notions of white supremacy, and as numerous others can attest, tribal communities sometimes still encounter these attitudes in local politics.

Tribal members resolutely resisted the temptation to respond to violence with violence. They were acutely aware that while the media would largely ignore aggressive actions by white individuals, any act of Indian violence would make headline news. This underscores a harsh lesson that tribes have had to learn about the realities of media coverage.

This case history provides an intriguing perspective on the roles of both federal and state courts. Despite both the tribe and its adversaries pursuing their objectives through litigation, the courts played a relatively minor role in the ultimate resolution. The County, the GCSD, the HOA, and Anderson secured victories in the Superior Court in El Dorado County, but these wins were overturned in federal courts. The tribe obtained federal appeals court affirmations of its sovereign status but experienced defeat in the local federal district court. In essence, the County emerged victorious on the local level, while the tribe fared better in courts and bodies beyond the immediate area.

It's not surprising to legal experts that geography can significantly influence certain judicial outcomes. Unfortunately, tribes frequently encounter hostile local juries and unsympathetic local judges.

Although litigation incurred substantial costs for both the tribe and its opponents, its primary utility and effectiveness were as a deterrent. In fact, one of the key factors leading to an agreement between the tribe and the county was a mutual commitment to avoid further court proceedings.

Once more, legal practitioners understand that ongoing or potential litigation can be a potent bargaining tool, and its expenses often play a role in negotiations. A crucial takeaway for tribes might be the significance of retaining highly experienced attorneys who possess extensive knowledge and practical experience in Indian law.

No other tribe in the United States has confronted the particular challenge of constructing a casino on a landlocked reservation, and this case history remains unique in that regard. Nevertheless, there are parallels with the contemporary experiences of many other tribes, both those aiming to establish a casino for the first time and those seeking to expand their gaming operations. Perhaps the most notable commonality is the experience of being compelled to make payments to state and local governments under the guise of project mitigation.

The tribe's relationship with CalTrans only improved after the tribe changed state law and made it evident that it was willing and capable of financing the exceptionally costly interchange project. Essentially, the tribe was coerced into agreeing to subsidize a significant component of the state's transportation infrastructure. This involved not only covering the expenses for the off-ramp providing access to its reservation but also funding 10 miles of High Occupancy Vehicle (HOV) lanes along Highway 50. Similarly, the County only reached an agreement when the tribe conceded to demands for subsidizing several of its major public programs and allocating funds for law enforcement and fire protection services.

The tribe complied with these substantial financial commitments because they recognized their position as the less powerful party in the negotiations. They understood that failing to comply would only result in continued growth of their ultimate costs and debt. This scenario is a common one for aspiring tribes looking to develop their tribal economies.

Another significant factor behind the tribe's agreement was their astute assessment that the political climate was turning against them. At that time, Schmit and the SUFC were capitalizing on a backlash against Indian gaming, and their push for subsidies to "compensate" local jurisdictions for gaming development was finding resonance among the people of El Dorado County. Similarly, Schwarzenegger's campaign for a "fair share" of gaming revenues, though partially countered by the Ventura ad, appealed to the public perception that tribes were reaping extravagant profits at the expense of tax-paying citizens.

This scenario underscores a clear lesson: as tribal negotiations with public agencies occur against the backdrop of shifting public opinion, the timing of negotiations often shapes the outcomes. Tribes must be equally well-informed about public sentiment as the officials they are dealing with.

Predictably, the tribe faced an increase in legal and financial challenges as more individuals grasped that plans for the casino were beginning to materialize. It was when it appeared that casino revenues would soon start flowing that the 'Historic Miwuks' and Anderson of Sharp Image launched their attacks. A negative ruling by a superior court judge at that juncture, before the casino was fully operational, could have pushed the tribe into financial ruin.

All gaming tribes and those on the verge of opening or expanding a casino confront a similar hurdle: local officials and their neighbors often hold highly inflated notions of casino profits. They also tend to exaggerate the crime and other negative consequences they believe follow casinos. To introduce a sense of financial realism into negotiations regarding "compensatory payments" and other subsidies, it is beneficial to disclose the true costs of initiating and maintaining gaming operations, which are not commonly known by elected officials. To counteract myths about crime and prostitution, it's advantageous to present factual evidence of tribal security's ability to maintain public order.

Shingle Springs encountered the challenge of being in the heart of a very conservative Republican county. They discovered that, regardless of their protections under federal law, they were highly vulnerable in front of local judges and juries. Even the local federal district court posed challenges. It was at this point that the tribe realized the absolute necessity of winning approval from local authorities by appeasing local opinion. Ideally, groundwork should be meticulously laid through a public education program well before negotiations commence with local governments.

Prior education of local opinion isn't just crucial for interactions with local officials but also for engaging with the local community and elected and appointed officials. As demonstrated in the Shingle Springs case history, federal officials also respond to local sentiment. The actions of officials in the BIA and NIGC reflected concerns that they might get entangled on the losing side of a local political struggle. The success of casino opponents lay in demonstrating the unpopularity of the tribe and its plans. This underscores the lesson that, even at the federal level, local majorities can wield significant influence. Once again, this emphasizes the importance of public education.

While they weren't the first tribe to engage with state agencies, the Shingle Springs Band became the first California tribe to discover that CalTrans did not recognize tribes as governments. Shingle Springs successfully pushed for a change in state law requiring this critical agency of the State of California to acknowledge and collaborate with tribes as tribal governments.

Perhaps the tribal leadership was initially optimistic in believing that state officials would remember or feel remorse over their 1965 decision to seize land for a road that blocked access to another part of the reservation. The agency's obstinate resistance to all the tribe's attempts to meet and discuss persisted despite the tribe's efforts to educate officials about their government status. Even when the Legislature passed a bill mandating coordination with the tribe, the agency remained unyielding, requiring intensive lobbying efforts to overcome the gubernatorial veto of the bill. This victory, hard-won though it was, imparts an important lesson: tribes must become effective advocates to protect their interests in legislative and regulatory politics.

Due to the efforts of Shingle Springs, other California tribes were recognized as governments and able to work with CalTrans on transportation projects without obstruction and obfuscation. Today, Caltrans and tribes up and down the state sit on local transportation boards and work together to bring improvements in local communities. This would not have been possible without the struggle and sacrifices from Shingle Springs. In a real sense, other tribes were the beneficiaries of the hard work and persistence of the Shingle Springs Band. In this way, victories won by one tribe become precedents on which others can later rely and bring improvements that benefit everyone in the community.

The Shingle Springs case history highlights the significance of leadership continuity within the tribe and the influential role of leading families on the tribal Council. Nicholas Fonseca served as chairman until 2007 and remained on the tribal Council, alongside Brian Fonseca, in 2020. Similarly, the Cuellar family, represented by Regina Cuellar and Pat Cuellar, continues to hold a major role on the Council. Annie Jones, a prominent figure in the tribe's leadership, has served on both the early and current Councils.

Notably, women have played a significant role in Shingle Springs' tribal leadership. Early Councils featured Annie Jones and Elaine Whitehurst, who organized local support groups and managed community relations. On the contemporary Council, women such as Annie Jones, Regina Cuellar, Pat Cuellar, and Jessica Godsey Olvera continue to make important contributions. Elaine Whitehurst remains involved with the tribe's economic development corporation to this day.

Strengthening Bonds: The Crucial Role of Community Outreach and Alliance Building.

In the intricate narrative of the tribe's journey to success, community outreach and coalition-building emerged as pivotal components.

Under the tireless leadership of Elaine Whitehurst, these endeavors transcended mere strategy; they symbolized the tribe's dedication to nurturing mutual understanding and shared visions. "We knew we had to engage with our neighbors and those who opposed us daily, building bridges to help them understand our perspective and the importance of our cause," concluded Elaine Whitehurst.

Whitehurst's leadership exemplified not only her skill in engaging various community factions but also her ability to comprehend their concerns, aspirations, and potential areas of collaboration. Guided by her, outreach initiatives evolved beyond traditional dialogues, transforming into platforms for exchange, learning, and unity.

Furthermore, the creation of a robust coalition of supporters underscored the tribe's proactive approach to bridge-building. Rather than passively seeking support, they took deliberate steps to involve potential allies, educate them about the tribe's objectives, and illuminate the mutual benefits of their collective efforts. This coalition became a potent advocate for the tribe's vision, amplifying their message to wider audiences.

In the larger narrative of the tribe's achievements, the community outreach and alliance-building led by Elaine Whitehurst not only served as strategic maneuvers but also as essential components in weaving a more inclusive, understanding, and collaborative future.

The conflicts witnessed in El Dorado County have not completely dissipated even with legally binding agreements. They have a prolonged impact. The County-Tribal MOU did not entirely silence controversy, the tribe's financial contributions to the County budget did not fully satisfy all local residents, certain unfounded criticisms against the tribe persist, and the grievances of some tribal members have not entirely faded.

Nevertheless, today, there's no denying that the Shingle Springs Band has emerged as a significant and highly respected player in the economic, social, and political life of the region. The tribe's commitment to improving community health and other facilities is steadily winning over local opinion."

Navigating Shared Challenges: Successful Strategies for Resolution

Unwavering Spirit: The Quest for Tribal Sovereignty Amidst Challenges

Throughout the 1990s and even into the present day, the advocacy for Indian casinos, despite achieving notable successes at the statewide level in California, continually encountered hurdles at local levels. The rich histories of tribes like San Manuel, Jamul and Shingle Springs, deeply intertwined with the land, remained largely obscured. An emphasis on educational initiatives illuminated the tribes' profound historical roots and the tragic narratives of dispossession. Interestingly, in some cases, these very localities supported Indian gaming initiatives more fervently than the state average.

As San Manuel, Jamul and Shingle Springs embarked on their casino ventures, they promptly initiated programs to showcase their positive impact on the community. It served as a poignant lesson that tribal projects necessitate groundwork to secure community engagement.

Nevertheless, local public sentiment represented just one facet of the challenge. The underlying obstacle was the deeply ingrained biases of local officials and that of some local residents. These officials, falsely viewing themselves as the definitive representatives of local majorities, often overlooked tribal sovereignty. Their treatment of tribes often mirrored their interactions with other property developers, failing to acknowledge the distinct challenges and federal rights associated with tribal land.

Tribes and corporate developers, although guided by distinct principles and histories, often found themselves ensnared in similar bureaucratic entanglements. Yet, while non-Indian corporations never encountered the unique challenges faced by tribes, the argument for treating tribes as ordinary developers persisted.

Paradoxically, the substantial financial contributions made by tribes unintentionally became a form of security. As these funds became integral to state and local budgets, a vested interest in the success of tribal gaming emerged.

Tribal ventures also faced opposition from two notable fronts: local residents concerned about disruptions to rural tranquility and vocal anti-gaming factions who frequently invoked moral and religious objections, painting a bleak picture of crime and vice associated with casinos. For tribes, they knew this was an area that demanded their immediate attention. The tribes met these challenges head-on, implementing comprehensive security measures, engaging in community outreach efforts, and establishing programs dedicated to addressing gambling addiction. In the end, the verifiable evidence lies in the statistics. The truth remains unshaken: none of the fears and disputes propagated by opponents of Indian gaming have come to fruition. Just consider this — when was the last instance you came across a news article detailing crime and corruption at a California Indian casino?

The key components of the tribes' recipe for success? A fundamental reliance on federal law and an unwavering commitment to pursuing a better future on a path to self-reliance. This relentless determination wasn't solely driven by economic aspirations but also by an intrinsic sense of responsibility toward past and future generations. It stood as a testament to the tribes' dedication to their sovereignty, a legacy passed down through generations that taught them resilience in the face of adversity.

As more women become active in tribal activities, it has a positive influence on the community. Many strong women are now making tough decisions and leading their tribes effectively. Remarkable tribal leaders like Lynn Valbuena, Erica Pinto, Mary Ann Andreas, Elaine Whitehurst, Brenda Soulliere, Rosemary Salgado, Audrey Martinez, Alexis Manzano, Carlene Chamberlain, Barbara Gonzalez, Michelle Salgado, Mary Belardo, Priscilla Hunter, Beth Ann Bodi, Annie Jones, and Rose Campbell all deserve recognition for their exceptional courage and unwavering determination to protect their people and tribal sovereignty. Their leadership paves the way for a brighter future in tribal gaming and beyond.

Tribal Elders

Tribal Elders hold a position of honor and reverence within Native American communities. They stand as the embodiment of ancient tribal wisdom and are celebrated for their unwavering commitment to securing a brighter future for their people.

These elders are not merely custodians of stories from the past; they serve as beacons guiding their communities forward. Through their narratives, they impart the struggles and triumphs of their tribes, igniting a flame of inspiration to carry forth their legacy.

Tribal Elders have dedicated themselves wholeheartedly to the well-being of their communities. They have weathered hardships, shared their invaluable insights, and nurtured the emergence of younger leaders. As esteemed mentors and beloved figures, they infuse unity, tradition, and purpose into their tribes, illustrating the enduring strength of Native American traditions and the lasting influence of tribal communities.

I am deeply humbled to have had the privilege of crossing paths with numerous tribal elders over the years. They have graciously afforded me the opportunity to gain profound insights into tribal life, instilling within me a deep appreciation for their unwavering commitment to future generations.

Tribal elders such as Santos Manuel, Carlene Chamberlain, Kenneth Mesa, Rowena Ramos, Pauline 'Dimples', Jim Adams, Louie Adams, Elaine Whitehurst, Annie Jones, Elsie Shelin, David Murray, Henry Duro, Jesse Pinto Sr., and Raymond Hunter have been instrumental in shaping the future of their tribes. These venerable figures risked everything for the dream of self-reliance and a better quality of life for the coming generations of their communities.

Among these extraordinary tribal elders and leaders, there was one individual who left an indelible mark on my heart — Pauline

"Dimples" Murillo. Her wisdom, kindness, and unwavering dedication were nothing short of inspiring. She served as a beacon of courage and leadership, guiding and inspiring countless individuals in shaping the future of San Manuel. Pauline's legacy will continue to thrive, carried forward by her loving family, and she will forever remain in our hearts.

CHAPTER SEVEN

The Future

"The best way to predict the future is to create it." Peter Drucker

There are hundreds of lessons and examples in this book. In this chapter, we embark on a comprehensive exploration across the nation, pinpointing a dozen pivotal issues that stand poised to shape the tribal landscape of tomorrow. With a keen eye on the horizon and drawing from a wellspring of expertise, we offer succinct yet effective strategies to navigate and address these imminent challenges.

Challenges to Tribal Sovereignty: A Contemporary Analysis

From the moment non-natives arrived in indigenous territories, tribal sovereignty has been under constant scrutiny and attack. Initially, the primary concern was land acquisition, the ongoing battle to buy back the reservation. Over time the focus shifted to concerns about tribal autonomy and sustainability. Despite the constitutional and legal guarantees for tribal self-governance, the question of sovereignty continues to be a significant hurdle for tribal communities.

Critics often dismiss tribal rights, considering tribal governments as lesser entities compared to local administrations. Such viewpoints ignore the tribes' legal standing and its unique relationship with the federal government. Unfortunately, this mindset reflects a widespread public mindset, forming the core of anti-Indian sentiment.

A new wave of envy has arisen, with non-natives resenting tribal economic growth. The new-found affluence of tribal members has been met with prejudice. There's a growing bitterness that tribal governments possess the means to fortify Native American communities and have much less dependence on welfare and external support.

Attacks on sovereignty, though varied, consistently jeopardize the economic privileges inherent in tribal independence. Sovereignty remains a cornerstone in disputes ranging from water and property rights to other rights non-natives routinely challenge. It's pivotal in debates concerning the transfer of land into trust and underpins discussions about public safety and tribal court jurisdictions.

Protecting tribal sovereignty often necessitates federal court interventions. Yet, fostering mutual understanding through education can bridge the divide between tribal and non-tribal communities. Enhanced communication, public awareness initiatives, and well-informed local governments can circumvent litigation costs. Recognizing the historical significance of tribal lands and acknowledging past injustices can foster community harmony.

It's essential for tribes to recognize that sovereignty paves the way for self-reliance. Elders bear the responsibility to educate younger generations about its significance. Inter-tribal bodies should prioritize sovereignty in their agendas, outreach, and interactions with official entities. Established tribes should also extend support to other tribes facing threats to their sovereignty.

Economic Diversification

Federal legislation establishes explicit guidelines governing the allocation of funds and the establishment of casinos by tribes. This complex framework is further regulated and overseen by federal administrative bodies.

Misconceptions often fueled by competitors and critics, can mislead local non-Indian communities into assuming that tribes operate without constraints and are free to do whatever they want.

Consequently, any new tribal venture frequently prompts the skeptical response: "OMG another casino?"

A significant obstacle to tribal economic diversification was San Diego County's policy, which for two decades banned local support on tribal land trust applications. This policy effectively hindered tribal land acquisitions, development, and expansion. The County Supervisors, perhaps influenced by Jamul's representative, uniformly opposed such requests. Over these years, there were no efforts to evaluate individual tribal projects or assess their potential merits; the County's response remained consistently no.

Significantly, this policy uniquely singled out tribal matters for restrictive treatment, establishing no equivalent limitations on any other demographic. In essence, it placed an undue burden on tribal communities, subjecting them to a set of rules and limitations not applied to anyone else in the county. This selective and restrictive approach effectively halted tribal development opportunities while leaving everyone else unaffected by such constraints. The 18 federally recognized tribes of San Diego County faced substantial challenges, both in terms of time and financial resources, when attempting to acquire new lands. County authorities indiscriminately rejected tribal initiatives encompassing housing, health-care, education, economic expansion, public utilities, and more, further compounding the obstacles they had to overcome.

This prolonged stagnation came to an end in 2020 when San Diego tribal leaders engaged with the newly elected majority of the San Diego Board of Supervisors. Following these negotiations, on May 5, 2021, the long-standing policy was repealed. A new directive was established, committing to collaboration with tribal governments and pledging to evaluate each project on an individual basis.

The catalyst for this change had two primary components. First, the tribes had, over the years, diligently fostered a reputation for responsible governance. Their significant roles as employers and contributors to the community, along with initiatives promoting safety, infrastructure, and diverse economic ventures, solidified their positive image. Moreover, strategic public relations campaigns emphasizing their contributions further bolstered their reputation as assets to the county.

Tribal Property Rights and Local Communities: Finding a Middle Ground

A prevalent misconception among local officials is that tribal entities are merely fronts for development corporations. While this perception may diminish as more local governments and communities face defeats in federal courts, deeply ingrained American beliefs in property rights will continue to stir tensions in tribal-local relations.

At the heart of most opposition to tribal casino constructions are neighboring landowners who firmly believe in their common law right to the peaceful enjoyment of their properties. These moments of contention often escalate, leading to public demonstrations and sometimes revealing racial prejudices. Media coverage of these disputes frequently portrays tribes as unsympathetic oppressors, fueling animosity and resulting in costly litigation.

Proactive measures by tribes can help mitigate these confrontations. Engaging in early community education about their history, culture, and intentions can foster understanding and goodwill. Addressing local concerns directly and, if necessary, negotiating with adamant landowners for property purchases can prevent potential conflicts.

It's worth noting that many communities have grown adjacent to tribal reservations, often unaware of their proximity until the tribe initiates a developmental project or seeks to reclaim parts of their ancestral lands. In such instances, tribes might consider property acquisitions, especially from those staunchly opposed to tribal initiatives.

It's essential for tribes to convey their deep-seated feelings for their ancestral lands, particularly when they've been taken away through deceit and manipulation. These tribes inherently value property rights, and by harnessing this shared understanding with local landowners and emphasizing the mutual benefits of development, harmonious coexistence becomes attainable. Building alliances based on mutual respect and understanding can pave the way for peaceful and mutually beneficial cohabitation in the same area.

Promoting Public Interest Initiatives: The Power of Tribal-Community Cooperation

While tribes maintain their sovereign prerogative over reservation development, they significantly benefit from securing the endorsement of their non-Indian counterparts instead of courting resistance.

Open dialogue and proactive education are key strategies. By familiarizing local communities with the history, culture, contributions, and legal status of tribal governments, tribes can dispel misconceptions. It's often advantageous to spotlight a tribe's enduring contributions to society, emphasizing the heavy toll of uninformed prejudices against the dividends of informed harmony.

Engaging local communities in tribal planning, showcasing mutual benefits, and emphasizing shared future aspirations can further dilute tensions. By committing to community welfare and integrating within local programs, tribes underscore their role as constructive partners in progress.

It's evident from numerous tribes that harmonious cooperation with local communities yields manifold returns. Many such communities rely on the generous philanthropy of tribal entities, fostering symbiotic relationships that benefit all.

In California, while three-quarters of the populace is affected in some way by tribal gaming, a significant number remain unaware of tribes' philanthropic endeavors in their communities. This gap underscores the potential of sharing such beneficial engagements.

Well-established tribes have discovered the boon of investing in broad-spectrum public interest initiatives. By sponsoring local charities, endowing scholarships, endorsing athletic endeavors, inaugurating sporting venues, and championing causes like environmental conservation, senior welfare, and health-care, they create a holistic impact. Funding first responders offers an especially tangible testament to the merits of tribal-community collaboration.

A prime exemplar is San Manuel's expansive health-care outreach. Beyond prioritizing its members' welfare, the tribe actively aids neighboring non-Indian communities, as evidenced by its alliance with Loma Linda Hospital to inaugurate a health-care center in San Bernardino. San Manuel, in partnership with Loma Linda University, also pioneered the San Manuel Gateway College, focusing on health-care workforce development — a much-needed initiative in today's health-care sector. This endeavor, coupled with extensive local media coverage, has earned the tribe immense local appreciation.

Simultaneously, tribes have mastered the art of balancing reminders of their inherent sovereignty with collaborative intergovernmental projects. Their endeavors consistently validate their self-governing capabilities while fortifying their stature as trustworthy partners.

The conclusion is inescapable: 'Public Interest' programs championed by tribes are a testament to the power of proactive communication. It's a lesson for the future: education isn't just beneficial — it's transformative.

Governance Dynamics and the Sovereign Essence of Tribal Governments

Tribes are independent sovereign nations. Native Americans view themselves as members of individual tribal governments, a view also held by the American founders. While tribes like San Manuel in California have distinguished themselves with an intricate structure of administrative, judicial, and regulatory entities, others face governance challenges that can not only detrimentally impact their members but also cast shadows on the reputation of tribal governments at large.

The autonomy of tribes in determining their governing structures is sacrosanct. An emergent understanding of effective governance practices offers guiding principles for tribes seeking robust self-administration. The concept of 'Best Practices' in tribal governance is gaining traction, especially among tribes involved in gaming and those diversifying their economies.

Historically, federal guidelines promoted a monolithic blueprint for tribal charters, advocating a universal model. This becomes clear when we look at how rules and ideas that try to make everything the same, both from the government and in studies, tend to ignore how different each tribe's history and culture really is.

It's imperative to underscore that tribes historically experienced distinct histories based on their geographical regions, each carrying its unique ethos of tradition, culture, and self-rule.

Yet, amid this diversity, there's an awakening among tribal leaders about the importance of inter-tribal consortiums at state and national levels. Recognizing the shared challenges and aspirations of Native Americans, there's a growing consensus on the imperative of cohesive political organization. After all, unity, while respecting diversity, remains a cornerstone for realizing collective aspirations.

Advocacy for Authentic Tribal History in Public Education

Many people don't know much about Native American history. But things are starting to change. Some states are realizing that it's important to teach students about real tribal history in school.

When these rules are put into practice, they need to be watched carefully. Take California, for example. In 1999, California said that local tribal history should be taught in schools. But, 20 years later, it was clear that something was missing. Important events, like the diseases brought by the Spaniards, the harm done to tribal culture in the Catholic Missions, the terrible things that happened in the mid-1800s, and how much land was taken in the 1900s, were left out. Thankfully, in 2021, the law changed to include these things, so now students can learn a more complete version of the local Native American history.

When people know the real history, it's not just about showing respect, it also helps to get rid of the wrong ideas and biases that exist today. Most tribal leaders aren't asking for payback for what happened in the past. They just want people to understand the truth: Native Americans were here first, and they lived here long before others came.

The rules that say tribes can make their own choices and be in charge of themselves, which are in the Constitution, should always be followed. People who aren't Native Americans don't need to give things back, but they should treat tribes fairly. When people understand the true history, they're more likely to support tribes' rights, especially their right to be in control of their own lives.

The Imperative of Understanding Federal Law in Tribal Contexts

Many Americans don't understand federal law. It's complex and often stays in the background, so they make no attempt to understand it. For the average person, federal law seems distant and only affects them once in a while, if at all. Federal law significantly shapes the lives of Native American communities, and its interaction with state laws plays a pivotal role in defining the realities for tribes.

Most people don't know how federal law controls tribal matters. This lack of understanding can lead to confusion, and sometimes even legal battles and protests against tribal groups. Part of this problem is that people don't know about the connections tribes have with the federal government and the rules set by Congress that affect Native American lives.

A lot of folks don't realize that their homes are on land that tribes historically claimed but were taken away by federal orders. The fact that tribes have their own sovereignty on these reservations, which is recognized by federal courts and approved by Congress, often goes unnoticed by the general public. When tribes announce projects, like casinos, it can come as a surprise and cause confusion or even unwarranted anger. Some people, without knowing the full story, jump to protest, sometimes without all the facts. The result can be a chaotic situation with legal fights, misunderstandings, and in extreme cases, violence.

But here's the twist: after all the legal and political battles settle down, some of the biggest opponents become strong supporters of tribal projects. Once they learn about the undeniable legal rights of tribes and see the economic growth and community improvements, they change their tune and back tribal businesses.

The big lesson here is crystal clear: knowledge is key. Tribes may avoid potential opposition by proactively teaching non-tribal communities about their rights spelled out in the Constitution and how these rights affect local government. Spending time and resources to explain federal law's complexities to local communities and leaders could ease resistance and clear up misunderstandings. When the public understands that tribal rights are protected by the Constitution, backed by Supreme Court decisions, and confirmed by laws passed by Congress, it might speed up tribal projects and maybe even reduce long-standing biases and community friction.

Teaching local leaders about the ins and outs of federal law is just as important. Local policymakers, like county supervisors and city officials, need to understand the basics of tribal sovereignty. Knowing that they have limited authority over federally approved tribal developments can lead to cooperation and help communities grow together through tribal initiatives.

Navigating the Complexities of IGRA Reform

While Congress and the federal courts are crucial in safeguarding tribal sovereignty, it's undeniable that certain federal laws, rooted in paternalistic ideologies, impose constraints on this sovereignty. A notable example is the legislative framework dictating how tribes allocate gaming revenues, placing restrictions on tribal endeavors in ways not experienced by any other ethnic group in the nation.

For over three decades, the Indian Gaming Regulatory Act (IGRA) has been a subject of scrutiny and contention. Critics have long called for its replacement, citing various flaws. A closer look at multiple case studies reveals the costly and counterproductive discord caused by IGRA, including tribal-state conflicts, inter-tribal discrepancies, and disputes with local governments.

IGRA isn't unique in its unintended consequences. Its designated regulatory bodies also have bureaucratic shortcomings. Reform advocates highlight IGRA's inherent bias toward affluent, established tribes and its inadequate enforcement of allocating gaming profits to non-gaming tribes. There's also a growing concern that tribal-state compacts are evolving into additional revenue sources for state and local administrations.

Yet, pursuing reform comes with uncertainties. Introducing new legislation might unintentionally strengthen the influence of well-established tribes and their influential advocates. While IGRA's flaws are well-documented, new legislation could bring unforeseen challenges. Moreover, the Bureau of Indian Affairs (BIA), despite its imperfections, is a recognized institution. Tribes have carefully adapted their strategies to align with established legal and regulatory benchmarks. Transitioning to a new legislative framework may require extensive adaptation, led by individuals unfamiliar with IGRA's historical context and evolution.

In essence, addressing IGRA's known challenges might be more advantageous than navigating the unpredictable terrain of a new legislative environment.

Tribes recognize that, despite its shortcomings, IGRA has played a crucial role in supporting their path to self-sustainability. It has improved governance, revitalized economies, enriched communities, and laid the foundation for brighter futures.

Championing Environmental Stewardship: A Tribal Legacy

Tribes often face criticism for their involvement in casino development and other economic ventures, with detractors accusing them of compromising environmental integrity. Tribal leaders view these criticisms with irony. Native Americans were the first champions of environmental conservation throughout history, embodying its principles long before the term "environmentalism" was coined.

For countless generations, Native American communities have practiced sustainable methods, achieving and demonstrating a delicate balance with the ecosystem. Today's urban sprawl and the consequences of commercialization make these accusations against them seem unfair and misplaced.

To address such misconceptions, tribes can proactively highlight their profound environmental values. By emphasizing their enduring connection with nature and their legacy of conservation, tribes can debunk many unfounded arguments against their economic pursuits. When communities understand the Native American commitment to the environment, it not only validates tribal projects but also portrays tribes as leaders in ecological balance.

Demystifying Tribal Governance: Sovereignty in Action.

Many non-Indians commonly misunderstand tribal lands, believing them to be lawless areas lacking governance, discipline, or regulation. They often remain unaware of the existence of tribal constitutions, detailed laws, and comprehensive regulations that govern each tribal nation. In California, it's important to note that local law enforcement has jurisdiction on tribal lands.

Contrary to these misconceptions, tribal governments uphold rigorous standards. Their economic activities, including gaming, undergo strict scrutiny from both federal and state agencies, and tribes have robust internal constitutions. These foundational documents are not mere formalities; they are essential in ensuring safety, equality, and ongoing opportunities for tribal members. For tribes, these constitutions represent a legacy for future generations, safeguarding the flame of tribal sovereignty.

It's crucial to address and dispel these misunderstandings. Tribes, especially those involved in gaming, can benefit from actively highlighting that their lands are governed by well-established legal frameworks. By educating the public and patrons about the thorough governance on tribal lands, tribes can alleviate doubts and instill confidence in their governance structures.

Confronting Prejudice: The Subtlety of Racism Towards Native Americans

Undoubtedly, in the pursuit of their goals, certain tribes have encountered a shadow of bias coloring their interactions. In the intricate realm of human prejudices, clear patterns of racism have occasionally surfaced. This stark reality becomes evident in public forums and meetings regarding tribal initiatives within local communities. Having personally attended hundreds of public hearings across the country, spanning highly contentious waste management landfill projects to major land development projects, I've encountered a level of animosity and fervor directed at Native American projects that surpasses even the most controversial non-tribal developments.

Racism is complex and often subtle. In modern times, few openly admit to harboring such biased views. Yet, it persists, sometimes lurking even within the hearts of individuals who may be unaware of their own prejudices.

Notably, the leaders of the tribes we've highlighted have chosen not to label their adversaries as racists or invoke the weighty concept of systemic racism. Instead, they strategically shine a light on the undeniable history of prejudice against Native Americans, refraining from igniting contemporary controversies.

In the court of public opinion, drawing attention to the historical injustices suffered by Native Americans carries significant weight. Modern tribes emphasize concepts like 'self-reliance,' 'economic independence,' and 'self-sufficiency.' Therefore, tribes generally exercise caution when accusing others of racism, reserving such claims for instances where it is glaring and indisputable.

While the call for reparations isn't a dominant voice, tribes primarily seek to have the unvarnished truth of history told. Their aim is recognition, not retribution. Today, the tribes' foremost aspiration is equality — the basic right to progress and prosper like any other community. For many Native Americans, a guiding principle might be: "Remember our past, never forget, but allow us to shape our future."

The Legacy of Sovereignty: Preparing the Future Tribal Generation

Education isn't just a means to enhance tribal relationships with neighboring communities or government bodies. It plays a vital role in nurturing understanding within the evolving fabric of the tribal community itself, especially among its youth.

Many elder tribal members carry memories of a time before the prosperity brought by casinos. They've endured severe poverty, encountered clear discrimination, and grappled with political and media biases. These experiences form the foundation of their understanding of the importance of tribal sovereignty, which is the cornerstone of their economic resurgence.

Some seasoned tribal leaders are becoming increasingly concerned that the younger generation may not fully grasp the essence of tribal sovereignty. This principle is not merely an abstract concept; it has been the driving force behind their economic achievements, setting tribal gaming apart from mainstream capitalism. The intention of tribal trailblazers has always been to instill an understanding of and respect for sovereignty in the minds and hearts of their successors.

Yet, there is a noticeable trend among some young tribal members to equate the tribe's operations with those of a typical corporate entity, believing that its success relies solely on conventional business practices. While their forebears certainly valued effective business skills, they also possessed a diverse skill set that encompassed advocacy, public relations, political strategies, and a deep knowledge of Indian law. The legacy they aim to pass down isn't just one of economic prosperity but also a comprehensive approach that upholds the tribe's distinct identity and rights.

In essence, the older generation hopes to ignite a sense of purpose in the youth — a commitment to preserving tribal sovereignty, ensuring that the tribe's legacy of self-governance and self-determination remains intact for future generations.

EPILOGUE

A Journey Heartfelt and Shared

As we conclude our exploration of these three tribes' intricate narratives, it's vital to consider the paths they've taken to achieve self-realization. Central to their stories are battles against misconceptions and stereotypes, highlighting the ongoing challenges faced by Native American communities.

These misunderstandings call for meaningful engagement and dialogue. Closing the comprehension gaps between tribes and their surrounding communities isn't just about dispelling myths; it's about nurturing mutual respect and collaboration.

Crucial to this effort is a nationwide push to embed an understanding of tribal sovereignty into our collective awareness. This isn't solely a matter of legal rights but an acknowledgment of tribes' historical role as independent governing entities, present since the nation's inception.

A broader acceptance and comprehension of tribal sovereignty will not only remove obstacles to tribal initiatives but also reveal the potential for a mutually beneficial relationship between tribes and the larger community. The way forward is marked by cooperation, mutual respect, and a shared vision of prosperity.

Thank you for allowing me to accompany you, even briefly, on this profound journey towards self-awareness and self-determination.

May you always find strength in unity, and may your aspirations light your path as you move forward. Take care, and may your dreams continue to guide you.

Rod

I trust you found the untold stories of Native American contributions enlightening and enjoyable. Please consider leaving a review. Both Amazon and Google welcome your insights, and you'll find links for each below—clearly labeled for your convenience.

While I'd be grateful for your feedback on both platforms, feel free to choose the one that suits you best. Your support in sharing your experience is deeply appreciated. Thank you!

Amazon Review

Google Review

Acknowledging the Indispensable

I want to express my heartfelt gratitude to the many individuals who have inspired my journey in writing this book. A special thank you goes to the leaders and members of the San Manuel Band of Mission Indians, the Shingle Springs Band of Miwok Indians, and the Jamul Indian Village of California.

I want to sincerely thank all the tribal members, elected representatives, and others who generously shared their time, insights, and experiences with me over the past three decades. While I cannot mention each person individually, I genuinely appreciate each one of you. I look forward to the chance to reconnect. Let's grab a coffee and catch up.

Throughout the last 30 years, I've had the extraordinary privilege of engaging with numerous seasoned professionals in Indian Country. Their wealth of knowledge on sovereignty, tribal governments, and tribal gaming in California, garnered through policy discussions and personal conversations, has significantly shaped my views.

I'm grateful to Carla Green and Clarity Designworks for their exceptional skills in book design, production, and publication, which have brought this work to life. I also owe a shout out to the PR Maestro, Peter Shankman, for his sage advice and introduction to Carla. Peter, your counsel has been invaluable, and for that, my friend, I am grateful.

I would be remiss if I did not personally thank my mentors and teachers who have helped shape me into the person I am today. Their ongoing wisdom and advice, counseling me to be curious and to push the envelope, have helped give a voice to many who otherwise may not have been heard.

Lastly, I cannot sufficiently express my deep appreciation for my family. Their unwavering support, encouragement, guidance, and steadfast belief in my capabilities have been my guiding light throughout this journey. Their faith in me has been unshakeable, their presence invaluable, and their love a source of immeasurable strength. It is a rare blessing to have such staunch champions in one's life, and I count myself fortunate beyond words for their presence in mine.

Why This Book? Why Now?

Dive into a world where history, strength, and today's realities come together: the world of Native American self-reliance, sovereignty, and Indian gaming. Are you ready to explore and learn, challenging what you thought you knew? It is time to tell these important unknown stories about Native Americans and their quest for self-reliance.

- **Unraveling Complexities:** This isn't just any book; it's an adventure into Native American life where traditions meet innovation, and progress is essential for survival.
- **A Journey to Independence:** Discover how Native American tribes use different methods to ensure their legacy lives on for generations. Learn how they've used things like Indian gaming to secure their future.
- **Understanding Sovereignty:** Tribal sovereignty isn't just an idea; it's a real part of Native American life. Dive into what this means and how it affects these communities every day.
- **Exploring Indian Gaming:** Beyond the glitz and glamour is an industry that's changed Native American economies. Find out more about Indian gaming, from its legal side to how it's transformed these communities.
- **Working with Governments:** Get a grasp of the delicate balance as tribal governments talk with federal, state, and local leaders.

In a world filled with misunderstandings, this book shines a light, leading you to deeper understanding and respect. If you're ready to be intrigued, informed, and inspired, this book is a must read. Witness the incredible journey of Native American communities as they strive for self-determination. It's time to understand. Come along for the journey.

Who Should Read This Book?

1. **Curious Minds:** Drawn to the Mystique of Native Americans? There's a rising tide of interest, with many now questioning their ties to tribal roots — a query almost unheard of two decades ago. Dive into a riveting exploration of Native American heritage and the nuances of Indian gaming. If you're keen to explore Native American history or the intricacies of Indian gaming, this book offers a compelling read.

2. **Tribal Economics:** Journey through the path of self-reliance taken by various tribes. A must-read for those keen to connect deeper with their heritage and understand the subtleties of Indian gaming and the challenges that lie ahead.

3. **Future Tribal Leaders:** Some say the next generation has become entitled with Indian gaming and dangerously complacent. Grasp the trials and tribulations of past generations and how you got here. Understand the legacy you inherit and debunk prevalent myths. Always prioritize the protection of tribal sovereignty, it's a legacy worth understanding and fiercely guarding. Rise to the occasion.

4. **Public Servants:** Many challenges have been born from false rumors, fear and a lack of understanding. Elected representatives, acquaint yourselves with the federally outlined processes for tribes and discover the unique narratives of the tribal communities within your jurisdiction. Let facts guide your decisions for the betterment of all. A genuine understanding

and respect for tribal governments can be the cornerstone to resolving local challenges.

5. **Members of Congress & Staff:** Equip yourself with the backstory for effective law-making. Understand the ripple effects and unintended consequences of legislation related to tribal matters and how that impacts local and state governments and the communities around reservations.

6. **Bureau of Indian Affairs (BIA) Personnel:** Dive deeper into the intricate challenges tribes face in their pursuit of self-reliance and the nuances of Indian gaming. This insight can enhance your grasp on the significance of land trust procedures and the heartfelt aspirations of tribes working to reclaim their reservations.

7. **Policy Makers:** Gaining insight into the tribal government's viewpoint can refine your decision-making, leading to more effective policies that acknowledge federal law and the constraints on tribes.

8. **State Leadership:** For governors and officials in states enriched by Indian gaming, this book serves as an essential compass to navigate and comprehend the full spectrum of the sector, offering a perspective that will enhance your collaboration with tribal governments.

9. **Scholars:** Dive into a pivotal resource tailored for courses on Native American history, sovereignty, or tribal gaming. This book provides a firsthand account of the defining moments over the past three decades, offering a unique lens into modern history.

10. **Journalists & Writers:** Engaged in covering tribal affairs or gaming? Dive deeper and equip yourself with nuanced insights. By crafting fact-based, rather than rumor-driven narratives,

you'll discover that approaching tribal leaders with understanding makes them invaluable allies and resources in the community.

11. **Social Justice Advocates:** Delve into the intersection of indigenous rights and social justice. Experience the powerful narratives of Native American communities in their unyielding pursuit for equality. A story waiting to be discovered, a fight demanding to be recognized.

12. **Gaming Enthusiasts:** Get a unique perspective on the gaming industry, particularly the role and implications of Indian gaming. Understand how your gaming dollars are making a difference in the lives of many in the community, not just adding to the bottom line for shareholders. Indian gaming is about people, not just gambling.

13. **Gaming Enthusiasts:** Dive into the world of tribal gaming. Here, every pull of a slot machine lever goes beyond mere entertainment — it resonates with the heartbeat of communities, uplifting real people and transforming lives every day. This stands in contrast to corporate gaming that is only focused on the bottom line for shareholders. Your money is making a difference. Thank you. Indian gaming extends beyond the allure of jackpots; it's a catalyst for empowering communities and fortifying a legacy for future generations.

This book goes beyond mere education; it shines a light on the profound challenges and pivotal forces that mold tribal leaders' choices. Get ready for an enlightening journey.

Key Areas of Investigation

- **Management:** Evaluating managerial styles, drawing observations from those who demonstrate a profound understanding of tribal perspectives, and assessing their capabilities in fostering long-term, sustainable growth.
- **Late entry into gaming:** It scrutinizes the challenges faced by tribes who made a late entry into the gaming sector.
- **Geographic Placement:** It examines how location can impact a tribe's gaming success.
- **Tribal Authenticity and Legitimacy:** It probes into questions around a tribe's genuine existence and its official recognition as a tribal government.
- **Sovereignty:** It addresses the impacts on tribal sovereignty resulting from various contemporary threats.
- **Regulatory Framework:** It investigates alterations to state and federal laws and the implications for tribal governance.
- **Financial Challenges:** It explores the financial struggles tribes face, the reasons behind them, and their effects.
- **Policy Failures:** It discusses official policy blunders and their repercussions for tribes.
- **Public Perception and Local Governments:** It considers how local governments and public opinion can shape tribal experiences.

- **Competition:** It assesses the competitive landscape, including other tribes and gaming interests.
- **Informal Powers:** It looks at unspoken influences on tribal dynamics.
- **Leadership and Politics within Tribes:** It delves into the role of leadership in tribal governance, the role of women, the operation of tribal democracy, and the impact of outsiders in tribal politics.
- **Inter-tribal and Intra-tribal Politics:** It addresses the dynamics within and among various tribes.
- **Organizational Structures:** It investigates the function of regional groupings, statewide, and national organizations in tribal life.
- **Coalition Politics:** It studies the role of alliances in furthering tribal goals.
- **Cultural Values:** It pays homage to the importance of elders and the preservation of tribal values.

Disclaimer

This book is for informational purposes only and should not be construed as professional advice. The author and publisher bear no responsibility for actions taken based on this content. All views are the author's alone. Seek expert guidance before acting on the book's content.

The information herein reflects the author's knowledge up to 2021. Subsequent updates are not included. The author is not liable for inaccuracies due to post-2021 changes. He has not received any compensation for this book and has solely covered all related expenses.

By reading this book, you agree that the author and publisher are free from any liability arising from the book's use. This work is not intended to replace expert advice in any field. All readers should consult professionals before making decisions based on this content.

The decision to write and publish this book was solely that of the author, uninfluenced by any tribe, individual, or entity.

The views expressed in this book do not represent the opinions or perspectives of Claremont Graduate University or the Drucker School of Management.

ABOUT THE AUTHOR

Meet Dr. Rod Wilson

With over three decades of experience working with Native American tribes, Dr. Rod Wilson is a trusted advisor, offering strategic guidance to tribal governments on their interactions with the public and with federal, state, and local governments. His firm conducts extensive research including surveys to measure public sentiment about tribal gaming and the other issues where tribal nations interact with other governments.

In this book, Dr. Wilson explores the significant challenges tribes face as they strive for self-reliance. He underscores the crucial roles tribal leaders assume in overcoming these obstacles, leveraging his extensive experience to offer invaluable insights that can improve outcomes and reduce conflicts within the broader communities.

Dr. Wilson serves as the Managing Partner and Co-Founder of a nationally recognized firm, specializing in communications, government relations, and marketing. His role in government affairs centers on orchestrating grassroots and media campaigns in support of important initiatives. Dr. Wilson is renowned for his adeptness in crisis management and project coordination, having conducted media and crisis management workshops across the United States.

His academic background spans a wide array of disciplines, encompassing political science, economics, government, and Artificial Intelligence. Dr. Wilson holds a Ph.D. in management from the prestigious Drucker School of Management. His steadfast dedication to advocating for Native American communities is evident in this book, reflecting his profound respect and unwavering commitment to the communities he passionately supports.

Made in the USA
Seal Beach, CA
28 September 2023

Made in United States
Cleveland, OH
04 November 2026

47645290R00133